A Season For Singles

Selected Meditations

Rebecca England
Peggy Haymes
editors

PEAKE ROAD

Macon, Georgia

ISBN 1-57312-048-0

A SEASON FOR SINGLES
Selected Meditations

Rebecca England
Peggy Haymes
editors

Peake Road
6316 Peake Road
Macon, Georgia 31210-3016

Peake Road
is an imprint of
Smyth & Helwys Publishing, Inc.

All biblical quotations are taken from the
New Revised Standard Version (NRSV) unless otherwise indicated.

Library of Congress Cataloging-in-Publication Data

From the Editors

If you're wondering about this book, let us tell you something about it. These devotions were written by married and single people. They address the particular aspects of living that many single people face, such as transition, solitude, commitment, facing challenges, practicing initiative, self-care, and learning to reach out. Of course, lots of these are issues that we *all* face!

Singleness is becoming more and more an accepted choice. Single adult departments of many churches are bursting at the seams with people of different ages who are looking for Christian community to share. No longer are we all in our twenties and looking for a mate. There are single parents, singles who have lost a mate to death or divorce, single working people who choose not to marry, handicapped singles. We don't need a dating service, we need a *church*.

The call of God is something that can take over and transform all other life commitments. Our status as Christians is more important than our marital status. When the word "we" is used in this book, it means "we followers of Jesus," and not "we single people." We hope this book provides for you comfort, challenge, and a sense of sharing community with other Christians!

Rebecca England and Peggy Haymes

A parable for living single or otherwise

Galatians 6:1-5

There were once two brothers who received an inheritance. One brother lived alone and the other brother had a wife and children. They each received equal parts of the inheritance and they worked together to bring a crop of grain from the land they received. When the crop was harvested, the brothers divided the grain equally. One evening as the married brother sat in his house with his family around him, he began to think of his brother. He thought to himself, "I have my wife and children to love me and take care of me, but my brother has no one. Who will look after his needs and help him in his old age? I must make sure he is taken care of." So the brother went in the middle of the night, took a sack of grain from his own storehouse and carried it secretly to his brother's storehouse.

The next night his single brother was resting peacefully at his own house when he began to think of his brother. He said to himself, "My needs are simple. I have only myself to take care of, while my brother has a family to provide for. I want to make sure they will have everything they need." So he went out in the middle of the night, took a sack of grain from his own storehouse and secretly carried it to his brother's.

The brothers continued their nightly excursions, carrying grain from storehouse to storehouse, each wondering how it was that the level in his own storehouse never went down. Until, inevitably, the brothers bumped into each other one night as they were carrying their sacks of grain. The brother's looks of surprise turned into smiles as they realized each other's secret.

Don't worry, be faithful

Psalm 37:1-9

❧ "What did you worry about a year ago today?" the roadside marquee asked.

It's a question worth asking on a regular basis. There's wisdom in the question. It reminds us that many of the things that we fret about, get heated up about, and lose sleep over are not worthy of serious attention. Yet we allow trivial things to rob us of the joy of our salvation and the power of our example.

"What am I fretting about today?"

"Why do I get heated up about things that have no long-term consequences, things that are just irritating?"

An worrisome spirit readily negates the fruit of the spirit: love, joy, peace, patience, kindness, generosity, faithfulness, gentleness and self-control (Gal 5:22-23). Today's reading gives us clear imperatives to counteract destructive attitudes.

- Do not be envious.
- Trust in the Lord and do good.
- Take delight in the Lord.
- Commit your way to the Lord.
- Be still before the Lord and wait patiently.
- Refrain from anger, forsake wrath.

Three times in nine verses, we find "Do not fret." Fretfulness is destructive and leads the Christian into sin against God, others, and oneself.

God of peace and assurance, forgive us for worrying about things that are not worthy of the worry. Give us the courage to be concerned about those items in our lives worthy of concern. From time to time remind us to be still and know that you are God. Amen.

2

Remember the outsiders

Isaiah 56:3-8

Eunuchs and foreigners. They were the ones with no rights, no place or privilege. Eunuchs were to be excluded from the covenant congregation as one of the "defective and impaired" people (Deut 23:1). Some foreigners were also barred from participation in worship, and their animals were not even deemed acceptable to sacrifice. Eunuchs and foreigners. The outsiders. The unacceptable ones. But not to God. For to those who are faithful, God promises a place "on the inside." God declares them welcome. God declares them accepted.

Who are the eunuchs and foreigners in your part of the world? Maybe it's those who are mentally or physically handicapped. Maybe it's the new wave of immigrants who bring their different language, culture, and ways of living to your city. Maybe it's the learning-disabled child who's labeled "the problem one." Maybe it's the elderly person who can't do as much or remember as much as she once did. Maybe it's the person with AIDS. Who are the outsiders? Isaiah reminds us that God does indeed hear their prayers as well.

Recently a friend shared with me the story of a young man who had joined their church. Dying of AIDS, he was already so weakened by the illness that he was confined to a wheelchair. The Sunday that he joined, he said to the congregation, "I turned my back on the church because the church had turned its back on me. But you have made me welcome."

God hears the prayer and honors the faith of all kinds of people, even those whom we would exclude. God's house has lots of room, enough even for eunuchs and foreigners.

3

Losing things

Matthew 16:21-28

I don't know about you, but when I lose things I go nuts until I find them. When word gets out that I have lost something, my family considers moving to the next state. I turn the house upside down. Regardless of the item's value I cannot rest until it is found.

Jesus calls me to do that which is my greatest fear, to lose something. It is even more distressing when I realize that I must lose the most valuable thing I have, my life or soul. Jesus does not speak of the physical life of our bodies continuing to function, but rather of the life that God has breathed into us at our creation.

In order to follow Jesus we must deny ourselves, which requires losing our lives. But, just to lose our lives for any good cause that comes along will not provide eternal profit for us. Nor can we, through hard work and dedication, achieve enough to exchange for our souls. A life lost for Jesus is a life that is found.

When I have something so important to me that I would panic if I lost it I always put it in a place so secure that not even I cannot find it. For many of us to be a part of the Kingdom of God means that we are "saved." Perhaps, we should say that our life must be "lost" in order to see the Kingdom. Maybe the question that we are to face is not simply, but what we are to give and how we are to give. To possess our very being we must not have it in our possession.

4

Coming home

Zephaniah 3:14-20

The ordination council convened at the request of the church for the purpose of examining the new associate pastor. The candidate had been a member of the church for over thirteen years. The church had witnessed her call to ministry, written recommendations when she applied for seminary, and then had chosen her to serve them.

One of the main fears the candidate faced as she attempted to discern God's leadership in accepting the call of her own church was what it would be like if their relationship soured and it became impossible for her to have the support that had been so instrumental in her nurturing. Would she be able to call this place "home"? She shared her concern with the ordination council.

The words of assurance she needed came from Paul, the council's chairperson. "This is God's church," he said. "You will always be welcome here."

Last winter the Dennis the Menace cartoon strip showed a crying Dennis in the arms of his mother. "I had to come home," he said. "I needed somebody to be on my side."

Whether facing the kids on the block, the possibility that out there somewhere relationships might change, or the Babylonian Exile, the need for home is crucial.

Advent calls our attention to God's need for a home for his own son. No room at the inn. A flight into Egypt to escape Herod's searching. A man without honor in his own country.

May God deliver us from the temptation to close the doors to our homes to those seeking refuge. Wherever we are, may it be known as a place where God dwells, and a place where all of God's children are welcome.

5

Forgiveness

Genesis 45:4-15

❧ What we find in our Scripture today is one of the most beautiful scenes in the entire Bible. Joseph, years before, had been sold into slavery by his brothers. His father had long ago since given him up for dead. Years passed and famine came to Joseph's family. The brothers came to Egypt for help in a time of grave difficulty. Here they encountered the brother they thought was dead.

Joseph, now a man of great power, did not cast them out. He did not turn them away empty-handed. With all the powers of the Egyptians behind him, Joseph did not punish his brothers. He opened his arms and forgave them and helped them.

Stop right now and think of your own story. Remember someone or ones who have made it hard for you along the way. Picture their faces. Say their names out loud. Pray for them and for yourself. If this is too painful, tell God how difficult you find this exercise. Pray that the power of your past hurts can find release. Pray for reconciliation.

Now read the Scripture lesson a second time. Let Joseph's story become your own.

Laundry

Isaiah 1:18-20

Recently a red sweatshirt of mine faded in the wash, staining several other pieces of clothing. Fortunately, nothing of value was stained, but another favorite sweatshirt did have to be relegated to "around the house" status. Some stains are like that. Despite our best efforts, our most helpful household hints, our newest and strongest cleaners, some stains are there to stay.

Have you ever had something like that in your life? You said the words that wounded another, the words that couldn't be taken back. You cheated on a test, or on your taxes, or misled someone in your family. You not only did not keep the promises that you made to God, but you callously disregarded them as you went about taking control of your own life.

We're sinners, all of us. Some of our sins are known to family and friends. Some of them we keep locked away deep within us. Some of them are easy to confess. It is hard to believe that we could be forgiven. Our sin stains the fabric of our relationship with God, and we fear that the damage is permanent.

But it's not so. These words from Isaiah remind us that there is no sin so dark that it cannot be forgiven, no wound so deep it cannot be healed, no stain so deep that it cannot be washed clean again. We are never "branded for life," unless it is by the sign of the love of God.

To read Isaiah to be reminded that forgiveness is no flippant affair. The God who forgives us and washes us clean also demands that we "cease to do evil, learn to do good" (Isa 1:16-17).

Limits

Isaiah 44:9-20

The idol shop was musty and crowded, only a few doors down the street from the local Buddhist temple. Matsu, Buddha, Kwanyin, and other gods made of ornate gold and silver stood in the corner ready to be delivered to the local temple. Wood chips and tools cluttered the floor of the tiny shop. I walked carefully to the back of the store to find the owner.

I saw a small Chinese man sitting quietly on the floor, legs crossed and hands poised in front of a huge block of wood. He was preparing to make a new idol. I watched as he worked. He picked up a tool with one hand and began searching for a place to cut. Then, with his other hand, he began to touch his own face. "Strange," I thought. He felt his nose, then the shape of his forehead, the curve of his lips. He slowly began to cut the wood, while, at the same time, touching his own face to find the right proportion and design. Later, he even stood in front of a small mirror and carefully studied his own facial features, looking for help in creating the face of this idol.

Idols, whether they are blocks of wood, stone institutions, brick homes, concrete opinions, or fiberglass boats, are designed by our own human hands. God is greater than all of these (Isa 40:45-46). The prophet Isaiah reminds us that sin is worshipping our own creation rather than the Creator. Idolatry sadly limits worship only to those things that we have created, and surely there is more to life than that. The question of the day is, What idols have you fashioned recently while gazing at yourself in the mirror? What limits have you placed on God?

Weeds

Matthew 13:24-30

In my backyard are great clumps of shasta daisies. In the winter, without the flowers, the green foliage resembles common weeds. One fall afternoon I set out to clean the debris from the summer garden. I began to dig with vigor, intent on digging every weed in sight. While halfway through the project, I looked down at the soil and gasped when I remembered. I had just dug up my beautiful flowers. I had been digging where tall, graceful shasta daisies had bloomed in the summer. And in my haste to clear out the weeds I had destroyed my beautiful daisy patch.

God plants good seed. Yet often weeds creep into the garden. It is natural for the servants in charge of the garden to want to clean out the weeds immediately. Who wants weeds in a beautiful flower garden? But the words from on high are, "Hold on a minute! You don't really know weeds from flowers. So you better leave both alone until the Master Gardener can take care of the garden."

I listen, but it is hard. I would really like a neat, clean garden plot, in accordance with my vision for the spring planting. Likewise, our natural tendency is to judge and place people in neat categories of righteous and unrighteous. Like the ancient Jew who understood clearly the categories—a righteous person obeyed the law, an unrighteous person did not—I, too, have categories. The irony of life is that often our categories do not fit. Righteous ones sometimes pluck grain on the Sabbath, eat with Pharisees, and have public conversations with immoral women. The lesson of the parable warns us that we better leave the categories to God. Only God can determine the truly righteous. Sometimes you and I can't even tell a weed from a daisy.

Little is much

Matthew 13:31-35

It is an important lesson of life—little is much. Creative writers will tell you while crafting words on a page that "little is much." Good cooks will tell you while using herbs and spices, "little is much." Clothing designers will tell you while creating a fashion statement, "little is much." Orators will tell you while preparing successful public speeches that "little is much." Great drama results from understatement. A slight look of the eyes creates a more vivid effect than a string of words used to explain the emotion. Little is much.

Why would we be surprised to consider that the mysteries of faith would be any different? True giant steps in the life of faith are not made from grandiose schemes of ecclesiastical ladder-climbing but from faithful, daily, sometimes even mundane tasks of faith. Leaps of faith are made in small steps.

True acts of piety really do not come from the ecclesiastical boardrooms or church business meetings where power is tossed to and fro but from the small acts of faith where quests for power are simply forgotten. For active faith refuses to be institutionalized. The small acts of faith can often reflect the true character of the gospel more than the large institutional ones. Praying while driving to work, stopping to check on a sick neighbor, calling a discouraged friend, playing in the sandpile with a child, silently pressing money in the hand of a friend who just lost her job, affirming a colleague, stopping to greet a newcomer, forgiving an enemy—little is much.

Discerning

1 Kings 3:5-12

Solomon stood on the front edge of his reign, and when God asked what to give him, Solomon asked for wisdom. "Give your servant therefore an understanding mind to govern your people, able to discern between good and evil . . ."

Perhaps it's a request we ought to make as well. For it's not always so easy to tell the difference between good and evil these days. Sometimes it's because evil looks so appealing to us—it's quick, it's easy, it's painless . . . or so it seems. Evil shines brighter and sings louder and promises more to us. At least for the moment. Good, on the other hand, can seem hard and painful, and painfully slow. Evil promises overnight results while good demands that we stay in for the long haul.

Sometimes it's hard to tell the difference, for we want to label as good those things that maintain our standing and our comfort level. We want to label it good if it confirms our prejudices and proves our points. For example, southern plantation owners vigorously argued (buttressed with biblical quotations) that slavery was a good institution. It made for a stable society and a healthy economy. The plantations wouldn't be nearly as productive without slaves, and then where would we be? The slaves were provided a place to live and a job to do. This was a good thing, wasn't it?

We humans have an enormous capacity for rationalization, for finding ways to justify ourselves and our actions. Sometimes we are even guilty of covering evil with a veneer of good, hoping that no one will be able to tell the difference.

And so, dear God, grant to us as well your wisdom, that we might be able to discern between good and evil.

Standing straight

Luke 13:10-17

🌀 It's a powerful image—a woman who has been bent over for eighteen years, unable to stand up straight.

The image is not altogether unfamiliar. For although many people stand up straight physically, emotionally and spiritually they spend years "bent over." Some are never able to stand up straight because they are carrying on their shoulders a heavy load of messages and wounds from childhood. "You'll never succeed . . . You'll never be as smart as your brother . . . Why can't you do anything right?" We are only beginning to learn the power that such childhood messages exert in our adult lives.

Others are bent over from a load of expectations that they can never quite fulfill. For example, many carry within themselves the expectation that they must sail through life perfectly, with never a hair out of place and never a mistake made. The ceaseless striving for perfection cripples them.

Some carry with them a load of rejections from their past—the relationships that ended, the marriage that failed. For still others the burdens come in the form of fears about the future. So anxious about tomorrow, they cannot celebrate today. And on and on our list could go.

What about you? What keeps you from being empowered to live your life fully, to make the best use of your God-given gifts? What keeps your hands tied and your soul bent over?

The Christ is here for us as well. He longs to heal us, to set us free from all that cripples our spirits. He sees us, not with the eyes of our own judgments, but with the eyes of love.

The Christ is here for us as well. Talk with him this day. Offer him your burdens, your fears, your wounds.

What matters

Matthew 13:44-52

When Furman University Chaplain L. D. Johnson died, the Asheville *Citizen-Times* published a eulogy entitled, "L. D. Johnson Knew What Mattered."

In one sense, that's what these two parables are about—knowing what matters. The treasure hidden in a field is worth more than all of his possessions. The pearl is worth everything he owns. What matters is not possessing many things of good value, but the one thing of greatest value. The Kingdom of God is more valuable than anything we can possess. It is worth the giving up of everything else in our lives for its sake.

What really matters in our lives? For what are we willing to sacrifice, to postpone immediate gratification in order to gain the greater joy of this thing which we value? For what are willing to give our very lives?

Perhaps the tragedy of so many lives is that this very question never gets asked. We run from one crisis to another, one bill to another, one vacation to another, never stopping to ask, what really matters? To what am I giving myself? For what am I trading my life?

For all of us are trading our lives for something. Day by day we give ourselves away. When we come to the end of our lives, will we find that we have traded them for a pearl whose beauty and value are beyond measure? Or will we find that we have exchanged them for fool's gold—shiny, insubstantial, and ultimately worthless.

When we speak of sacrifice in regard to our faith, we always focus on what we are to give up. But Jesus reminds us in these parables that what we give up is small indeed in comparison to the treasure we gain.

Marketing

John 6:35-40

❧ "Nothing personal, Jesus," the image consultant said, "but we've got to polish up your image a bit."

And Jesus said nothing. But the consultant didn't notice and continued on.

"Take for example, all this business about bread and hunger and thirst. Nice touch, real homey. But you gotta understand, Jesus, it doesn't have much pizzazz. It doesn't reach out and grab you. Now work with me here. What about, 'I'm the eight-course meal'—let them know they're really getting a deal." But Jesus said nothing

"Come on, Jesus, you're not working with me. We've got to have something that sells. If you're committed to this water concept, that's okay. That's good. Water is in. We could promote you as the imported mineral water sort of fellow. You know, goes down easy and is good for you." But Jesus said nothing.

"Listen Jesus, we're not going to get anywhere if you insist on holding on to these common, old-fashioned images. Virtual reality—now there's the ticket. 'I'm your virtual reality.' Has a nice ring, don't you think?"

But Jesus said nothing, for he was looking out the window. And there he saw crowds of well-dressed executives hurrying to their meetings, hollow inside. And he saw workingmen going about their jobs, covering over their emptiness within. He saw parents pushing children in strollers while they tried to push away the knots in their souls.

He winced and he sighed, for in that moment he heard their sighs that they swallowed along with their dinners. He felt the ache that they washed down with their drinks. They didn't need someone to impress them. They needed someone to fill them.

And Jesus said, "I am the bread of life."

Compassion

John 15:12-17

Again, look into the eyes of Jesus and you can see God. Look into the eyes of Jesus and you can see the people of the world. Look into the eyes of Jesus and you can see passionate love for God. Look into the eyes of Jesus and you can see passionate love for people.

Those eyes are not the glazed-over eyes of those who relish their private love affair with God. They are not the eyes of the self-righteous, self-appointed religious generals who wage holy battle to identify the sheep and goats. They are not the eyes of the passive individual who thinks that religion is a nice idea. They are the eyes of passion. They are the eyes with outreaching arms, an open heart, with feet ready for action. They are the eyes of love, not sentimental, not judgmental, not self-serving, not private versions of "love." They are the eyes of God's love. They are eyes of sparking anger when "the least of these" are mistreated. They are tear-filled eyes for God's little ones who grieve. They are laughing eyes celebrating small accomplishments. They are understanding eyes for those confused. They are eyes of hope for those who are despairing. They are compassionate eyes fixed in sockets of holy passion.

That's what it all comes down to. A passionate faith yields compassionate persons. Passionate love for God yields compassion for people, true compassion which responds to others, willing to risk misunderstanding, willing to appear inconsistent, willing to be labeled "odd" or "peculiar."

[Jesus' passion] was a focused passion. It was a passion directed to loving God and as a result passion directed toward caring for people.

— From David N. Duke, *Anguish and the Word* (Macon GA: Smyth & Helwys, 1992) 100-101.

Abundance

John 10:1-10

Hal Warlick tells the story of a schoolteacher who saved for many years in order to take a luxurious cruise. The day finally came, and she set off on her vacation on the fine ship. During the course of the cruise, however, she was discovered eating peanut butter crackers in her room. No one had told her that the food was included in the price of the cruise. There were meals morning, noon, and night—banquet tables groaning with every good thing. But alone she ate her peanut butter crackers. She didn't know she had a place at the feast.

What a telling parable for our lives. Jesus comes to us bringing life. Not a drab sort of barely existing, but life that is abundant, full and deep. Jesus offers to us a gift of life far grander than anything we could imagine for ourselves.

He doesn't offer us riches and wealth, but a richly satisfying relationship with the One who created us. He doesn't offer a guarantee of smooth sailing, but a life-giving abundance called faith. He offers us the chance to be all that we were created to be, which is always far more than we could dream. There is much in our lives that would kill our spirits, steal our joy, and destroy our hopes. But Jesus comes that we might live, and have it abundantly.

Forgive us, O God, when we measure out our lives in careful teaspoonfuls, when our lives are small, petty and pinched—anything but abundant.

Help us, O Lord, to leave our cabins and our peanut butter crackers behind, and to join you great feast. For it's where we ought to be, where we truly belong. Help us to accept your gift with glad hearts and laughing spirits. Amen.

Brother Tempest

John 14:8-14

Ever hear of Brother Tempest?

He is a wonderful Mexican priest featured in a 1987 *Sports Illustrated* article titled "A Ring and a Prayer." In order to get money to keep his orphanage going, this priest took a second job . . . as a *professional wrestler!* His "ring name" is Brother Tempest. His favorite hold is the dreaded "confessional." Every time the good padre gets an opponent in his "confessional" hold, the crowd roars "Repent, sinner!"

This kind, forty-two year old priest houses over eighty-six orphans in a dilapidated building with only one hole in the cement for a toilet. He is diabetic, overweight and really shouldn't be "wrasslin'," but he does it for the kids. The children are runaways, drug addicts, children of prostitutes, and abandoned children. One youth, age fourteen, had slept in a subway for two years before he heard of the wrestling priest's orphanage and begged enough money to get there. The only toys are worn-out tires. Breakfast almost every day is refried beans, tortillas, and half a cup of powdered milk. When a promoter sends the padre plane fare and hotel money for an out of town match, the priest saves the money by driving, even if it means thirty-four hours round trip and sleeping in his car.

The story describes the weary priest's face as he removes his costume mask after a late match and a long trip home. It concludes, "If he were here today, trying to keep eighty-six children warm and fed and off the streets, would the face of Jesus look very different?"

The face of Jesus reveals the face of God. Our faces and presence, as we do his work, can reveal the face of God to others.

Surprise

John 4:19-26

John Claypool, one of America's outstanding preachers, is often heard to say, "God's other name is surprise!" That is precisely the lesson that Jesus intends that we learn from his story of his encounter with the woman at the well.

While the theme of surprise runs throughout the story, it is nowhere more jarring than in the woman's discovery about worship. If the Samaritan woman is certain about anything, it is about where God is to be worshipped. She has no doubts. God is to be worshipped in the way and in the place where generations of her ancestors have worshipped God. Jesus steps into the life of the woman at the well to totally rearrange her perceptions about the worship of God.

By means of this story, Jesus invites us to examine our assumptions about the worship of God. Are we missing dimensions of God by the assumptions and routine of our corporate and private worship? A witty character has written that the seven last words of the church are "We never did it that way before." Those are certainly the seven last words of worship as a means to discover the greatness and diversity of God. Let this text from John invite you today to seek new ways and places to find and worship God.

"I am about to do a new thing; now it spring forth, do you not perceive it?" (Isa 43:19a).

Saying no

1 Peter 5:6-11

Do you remember the old proverb "An ounce of prevention is worth a pound of cure"? Prevention's goal is to fulfill lives. Part of its process is saying no to unhealthy things. Saying no to drugs, for example. But we continue the process of leading healthy, fulfilled lives only by saying yes to positive things. Saying no to something doesn't guarantee saying yes to a better thing.

That's where "prevention as physics fits." Prevention educator Carl Shanzis describes prevention along the lines of a law of physics: two objects cannot occupy the same space at the same time. A person ingrained with positive behaviors and attitudes won't have much room for negative behaviors and attitudes to creep in. Luke 11:24-26 exemplifies prevention as physics. Someone said no to this evil spirit living in her, yet when the spirit came back around the old neighborhood it found the place spic and span and better than ever to live in. The place was so great that the spirit brought along a bunch of friends. The person didn't fill the space.

Preventionist Peter teaches, "Be on the lookout. Pay attention." He doesn't simply mean for us to look over our shoulders waiting for something awful to happen. He wants us to looking to the living God and experiencing God's goodness. If we accept God's grace, then we can reject unhealthy things in life. We experience God's grace by placing our lives and wills in God's care. God as physics, so to speak

Home

Revelation 21:1-4

Who has not dreamed of it alone in the night? Who has not whispered the hope of it to their souls? Who has not longed for the coming of such a day?

No longer will the family gather awkwardly by the bedside, holding on to love while their loved one lets go of life. No more helpless waiting while disease ravages the body or makes useless the mind. No more angry frustration with inexplicable suffering. No more painful questions that have no answers. No more children dying before they've had a chance at life, and no more adults living long after their lives have ended. No more pain to batter our hearts; no more anguish to wrench our souls. Who has not longed for such a time?

In those days, perhaps there will be tears. But it will be the tears of laughter and the weeping of joy. And for those who come with sorrow's tears still fresh upon their faces, gentle hands strong enough to form a world will wipe their cheeks and dry their eyes. Who has not longed for such a day?

That day comes, not with charts or timetables or schedules of our making. That day comes in its own way and its own time. Who can say how such a time will come? Its coming is wrapped in as much mystery as promise. That it will come at all cannot be proven. But still faith whispers the dream in our ears.

In that time, the family will be united, and God will once again walk among us. We knew it only as a dream, a hope, a half-uttered prayer. But in that time our hearts will know the truth of it. We will be home.

Being remembered

Psalm 9:11-20

"Don't forget me," the new friends say as they leave summer camp. "Don't forget me," she thinks as she watches him board the plane for a year overseas. "Don't forget about us," the parents say only half-jokingly as their child leaves for college.

Don't forget me. Recently, I returned to my old high school to attend my niece's band concert. It had been years since I'd walked those halls, but when I saw my old softball coach I introduced myself to her (I had changed a little since tenth grade!). She immediately hugged me and said, "Of course, you played softball." It was nice to be remembered.

There is something in all of us that hungers to be remembered. If you doubt that's so, visit any nursing home and see the scores of people there who long for someone to remember that they exist, to remember who they are.

Don't forget me. It is the cry of a child to a divorced parent. "Now that you no longer live with me, please don't forget me." It is the cry of the sick and the homebound. "Now that I can no longer get out, don't forget that I'm here."

Don't forget me. In the deepest levels of our souls, it is a cry to God. Especially if we are in pain or difficulty, we cry to our God, "Remember me."

This psalm celebrates a God who does not forget God's people. Even in times of distress, God still remembers the afflicted, the suffering. Those who turn away from God and who forget God, God abandons to the logical consequences of their sin. But God will not forget those in need. God will remember the people of Israel. God will remember us.

21

Exile

Micah 4:8-10

In these three verses, we have both pain and promise, exile and redemption. Israel will be taken to Babylon, and her pain will be like that of a woman in the midst of a hard labor. But God will not forget Israel. The time of birth will come, and Israel will be redeemed, returned to her home.

When I was in grade school, I had a Spanish teacher who had fled from Cuba during Castro's revolution. A professional in his homeland, he'd had to leave most of his possessions behind.

Most of us have not had the experience of that kind of major dislocation, to be physically exiled from home and family and all that is familiar. But still we know about exile.

We know about those times when we feel like a stranger in our own homes. Nothing is right; nothing fits in our lives anymore. We feel cut off from all that once brought comfort and strength. We are in a strange land, knowing neither the language nor the customs.

Sometimes the exile is of our own making. We choose pathways that we know are not the ways of God. Is it any surprise then, that we wake up one day in a foreign land?

But sometimes the exile is forced upon us. Illness cuts us off from our normal routine. We can no longer do those tasks that once came easily or even gather with the community of faith for worship. And we feel isolated. Or we are laid off from our jobs; cut off from the community of the employed.

However it comes in our lives, we know about exile. Let us hear the word of promise and hope as well. God will remember. God will reach out to redeem us, even in a far land.

Success

I Cor. 4:8-13

A few people cough nervously as he wanders in late to the alumni meeting. They're dressed well, wearing the best they have. After all, now is the time to show your peers that you've made something of yourself.

But this fellow is different. His clothes are worn and torn and patched and dirty. His classmates don't know whether to feel sorry for him for not having any better or for not knowing any better.

His nose, never small to start with, shows signs of having been broken a time or two. His right eye still carries a deep purple smudge, and there are stitches across his left cheek. He grimaces a bit when he stands, as if the effort is painful. His classmates mutter to each other how awful it is that he's let himself go like that.

As a part of the meeting, they read out a list of awards alumni have won, offices they've been elected to and places of honor they've filled. It's how they keep up with what everyone is doing these days. To no one's surprise, no one calls that poor fellow's name. And when the time comes to elect new officers, no one nominates him to serve. It's obvious by looking at him that he just isn't the kind of person to sit on a board or be asked to preach at the annual convention. Besides, the word is that he has a bit of a temper that could turn nasty.

When it comes time to fill out registration forms, Paul has to leave the address line blank. He's homeless.

In school, his classmates said, Brother Saul/Paul had just as much potential as anyone. It's a shame that he never made much of himself.

Replenishing

Matthew 25:1-13

In reading this parable recently, I was struck by the theme of replenishing. All ten of the maidens had lamps which burned low but only five of them had extra oil with which to replenish their lamps. As a result, they were the only ones present when the bridegroom arrived.

It is dangerous for a church, as well as an individual, to become focused only on itself. To be solely concerned with your inward journey is to live an unbalanced life of faith—there must be an outer journey as well.

But the reverse is also true. If we fail to cultivate the inward disciplines of prayer and study, meditation and reflection, we wind up like the foolish maidens—running out of fuel.

If we are to reach out to the needs of this world, if we are to develop and use our gifts, if we are to follow God's calling in our lives, there must be times for replenishment. It may be a daily time for prayer and study, it may be time away on retreat.

One of the ways that I replenish is to visit a retreat center in a nearby city. There I am free to walk through the woods, listening to the silences. The staff prepares wonderful, healthy meals to feed my body while times of quiet in the small chapel feed my soul. Whether I am there for a day of for a weekend, I always return refreshed and replenished.

In the parable, it is the maidens who have the oil with which to replenish their lamps who are the ones who are present to greet the bridegroom. So it is with us that as we replenish our spiritual lamps, we are present and available to welcome our Lord.

Dry spells

Isaiah 12:1-6

Writers sometimes speak of hitting "a dry spell," a frustrating time when nothing good and creative seems to come to the surface. Indeed, all of us know something about such times. The challenges that we once relished at work become simply annoyances. The relationships that brought us joy now seem empty.

We know of such times in the life of faith as well. "The dark night of the soul," St. John of the Cross called it. Perhaps it comes to us with the suddenness and force of unexpected tragedies in our lives. Or perhaps it simply creeps up on us until one day we realize that the hymns that once brought us joy are merely notes, the prayers in which we once found strength are now merely words. Mechanically we go about our worship, or perhaps we cannot worship at all. There seems to be no answers to our questions, and no morning for our night.

In such times, the word that the prophet brought to the people of Israel becomes a word to us as well. God is our strength and salvation, Isaiah proclaims. Trust in God, and the day will yet come when our dry faith is refreshed by the cool, clean waters of the wells of salvation. The day will come when we once again give thanks. Once again, we will sing for joy.

Sometimes the best word that faith can offer is "Trust." What has been will yet be again. Although there is not yet a sign of dawn on the horizon, wait with hope, for the dark night will not last forever.

If you are facing such a time, remember the words of this prophet, written during dark and dry days. I will trust, and I will not be afraid.

Soul hunger

John 6:35-40

Have you ever been hungry? I don't mean a stomach growling at 11:55 on Sunday morning but a real hunger that distracts you so much that all you can think about is satisfying it.

Have you ever been thirsty? Not the kind of thirst where you stop for a drink to wash down your bag of peanuts, but the kind of thirst that makes your mouth dry and your throat raw.

Some of us never know true hunger and thirst. We keep filling our bodies with so much junk that we never have the chance to feel what we are really craving.

Have you ever been hungry and thirsty? Not just in the way of the flesh, but also in the way of the spirit. Have you ever felt a hunger for something deep within that you could not even name? Have you ever felt the dryness of your soul reaching for some refreshment that seemed just out of reach? Have you ever felt a longing for something more in life than what could be seen or touched or plotted on a graph?

Some of us never know the deepest hungers of our soul because we have been so busy filling our lives with a kind of junk food. We keep ourselves busy with things to do and things to worry about, and we never stop to listen to what is growling within us. We lose ourselves in an endless round of television shows that numb our spirits so that we don't have to feel the longing.

"I am the bread of life," Jesus said. May we live in such a way to discover that authentic hunger within us, and then may we seek the One who satisfies the longing of our hearts.

Choices

John 6:66-69

A local restaurant is a particular favorite of mine. I've been there so often, I have the routine of ordering down pat. Not waiting for the waiter's questions, I say, "I'd like a cheeseburger, cheddar cheese, medium rare, whole grain bun, potato salad."

There are a lot of choices to make, and not only in ordering a meal. We live in an age of choices, from the type of heating system for our houses to the stereo system in our cars.

But deeper are the choices as to what and who will claim our allegiance, how we will live our lives and for what end. Browse through a bookstore, and take note of all the books proposing choices for our lives.

Some people made a choice about Jesus. They had been glad to follow him for a while. But now he was talking strangely. His words were difficult and hard to understand, and they weren't sure that it was worth the trouble. They quietly slipped away, went home to await the next messiah.

"Are you going, too?" Jesus asked the disciples. "Where else shall we go," Peter answered. "You have the words of eternal life."

In the long run, it doesn't matter much whether I choose potato salad or pasta salad as my side dish. What does matter is who and what I choose to follow. There are many who may promise peace of mind or success in life and business.

But there is only One who promises us not a way to get ahead in life, but life itself. There is only One with the power to quench the deepest thirsts of our spirits and the deepest hungers of our hearts.

Where else shall we go?

Middle times

Romans 13:11-14

The preacher caused a stir by announcing that he had figured out the precise time of the Lord's return, and the time was at hand. Some people gave away possessions. Some waited with eagerness, others with skepticism. The appointed hour came and went with no triumphant return. And for many people, life went back to normal.

The early church lived in constant anticipation of the imminent return of Christ. Life in the present was lived differently because they believed that in the near future Christ would return. But nearly two thousand years later, we still wait. We don't know if Christ will return in our lifetime or another. How should we then live?

The words of Paul still apply to us. With the advent of Christ, the kingdom of God has broken into this world. With the return of Christ, the kingdom will finally come. We live in the in-between times, but we live looking towards the future. Already we live as citizens of that new kingdom. Whether that kingdom is to be realized tomorrow or a thousand years from now makes no difference in the way we live. Already we live as those who bear the name of Christ, who have chosen to follow the way of Christ.

We are not guided by the ways of this world, ways of selfishness and greed. We live in the way of Christ, in the way of love.

"What would you do if you knew Christ was coming back today?" the radio preacher asked. For the Christian, regardless of the hour, the answer is the same, "Love the Lord my God with all my heart soul, and mind . . . love my neighbor as myself."

Waiting

Psalm 80:1-7

Talking with people who are going through difficult days, I often encourage them to read the psalms. Not so much to find words of assurance and comfort, though those words are there for us. Rather, it's because in the psalms we find all of the honest emotion of the human experience.

There are psalms of deep faith and trust; there are psalms of celebration and joy. But there are also psalms that are more cries than hymns, psalms that rise out of the deep, dark places of our souls.

Such is this text. The people of Israel cry out for God to save them from their enemies. But here is no politely embroidered, delicately engraved request. Instead, they cry with the urgency of their suffering. "How long (a favorite phrase in the psalms) will you let this go on? Haven't we had enough?" God sustained the people of Israel with manna in the wilderness, but now they feed on "the bread of tears."

Have you ever felt that way? Maybe your circumstances were different, but have you ever wanted to shake your fist to the heavens and shout, "How long, O Lord? Haven't I had enough?"

"I don't know if I could tell God what I really feel," people sometimes tell me. And I tell them to go ahead, for God is big enough to handle our anger, God is compassionate enough to hear our cries. And God's love is deep enough and broad enough that we will not dam up its flow by our honesty.

Be honest with God this day, with your doubts and your gratitude, your fears and frustrations and anger and hope. And know that the same God who heard the cries of the psalmist, who sustained the people of God, hears your prayer as well.

Silence

Luke 1:5-25

In New Zealand there is a famous cave known as the cave of the glow-worms. One enters in a boat pulled silently through the water. The visitor sees a soft glowing light in the distance. From the top of the cave thousands of threads hang from the glowing worms. The cave has a fairyland appearance. The light is so bright one can read. But if there is the slightest noise the light dims, as if a switch were turned off.

If we wish to grow closer to God and be guided by divine light we must seek silence, a rare commodity in this noisy world. We are constantly bombarded by sounds of all kinds. But silence is essential if we are to hear the still small whisper of God's voice. We have to be deliberate in our praying to create silent spaces in which God can speak to us. We have to learn to "shut up" so we can hear. Only in silence can Advent truly be a time of preparation for the coming of the Christ child.

Zechariah, in his encounter with Gabriel in the sanctuary of the Lord, had a kind of silence thrust upon him. He certainly didn't seek to be mute, but for at least nine months he said not a word. Perhaps in his silence he turned his heart toward God and became more open to God's voice. Perhaps Zechariah used his temporary handicap to allow God to speak to him more clearly. When he finally spoke, his first words were in praise of God (v. 64).

Let us pray that we will hear God's invitation to silent communion so our hearts may be filled with Christ-love as we prepare for Christmas.

Speaking up

Amos 5:10-15

As a social worker in an agency serving those known as "the working poor," I was privy to information about pay scales for entry level and semi-skilled jobs in major corporations in my city. There were one thousand families on the waiting list because the parents' full-time wages were too low to pay for the day care they needed. These parents and children needed a prophet like Amos.

The prophet's criticism is against structural oppression, since there is a relationship between the poor who have been cheated and the rich who have gained from unfair business practices. And the curse upon those with economic security is that they will not have the joy of their possessions because the means of acquisition was wrong.

When cheating, bribery and public injustice seem to be the order of the day, a cautious person is often silent. Apathy and passivity are tempting simply because they require no effort. But a prophet is not prudent.

The word that comes from God at such a time must be said. The word from Amos is: "Don't just sit there!" It is not enough to avoid personal sin; the common good must be sought. Evil must be hated and justice established in all the gates of public life.

A favorite saying of justice-seekers is a summation of this passage: All that is required for evil to triumph is that good people do nothing. To be silent is to be an accessory.

What then should we do?

Suffering

2 Timothy 1:8-14

Perhaps it is only human nature to recoil from Paul's theme in this passage. Of course we are not ashamed of the gospel, but suffering for the gospel is surely an unpleasant matter.

Timothy is getting a dose of reality testing from his teacher. It is a living witness of the gospel which is so forthright that to be imprisoned is not a matter of shame but of dependence on God's grace.

Can we truly imagine our own response to Paul's invitation– "Join with me in suffering for the gospel"? Paul's reasons fly in the face of our illusion of self-sufficiency. The grace of life in Jesus Christ cannot be earned, but only accepted.

Even without a Damascus road experience, we have all been appointed as heralds, apostles and teachers. Therefore we are at risk of suffering. Paul defies the gospel of prosperity and success.

I am grateful to belong to a church community where suffering in public is not a matter of shame or scorn. This permission, which Paul is trying to impress on Timothy, makes it easier to be a whole person rather than one person in real life and another person at church.

The forbearance required of us is a matter of faith. Trusting in the grace of God is a spiritual habit, not a matter of a few lucky moments.

According to Paul, we have had the treasure of the gospel entrusted to us. And we have been given the Holy Spirit. the Comforter, as a companion on the way.

Thus we will learn, day by day, that nothing crucial in our lives happens without the baptism of tears.

Barriers

Ephesians 2:12-22

In 1989, a friend bought me a souvenir piece of the Berlin Wall. In my youth, I apprehensively watched black and white newsreels as the wall went up and tensions mounted. As an adult, I watched the destruction of the wall on live TV. The change in media wasn't as significant to me as the change in international relationships. The Berlin Wall stood all those years as a "dividing wall of hostility." The city was divided with concrete walls, barbed wire, and armed guards who shot to kill. The penalty for attempting to escape from East Berlin was death. The wall stood also as an ugly symbol of the hostility between Communist and Democratic countries. It was a sign of the enmity that sin causes in our world.

There were walls in the temple in Jesus' day. There was a wall to keep the Gentiles out—the penalty for crossing it was death. There was a wall to keep women from getting too close. There was a veil inside the temple to keep even the priests from coming too close to the Holy of Holies. The commandments and regulations of the law required the walls and the veil. When Jesus died on the cross, the veil was torn in two from top to bottom. Not long afterward, the stone walls came tumbling down.

Jesus destroyed the barriers. He made one people out of many. He ended hostility. He reconciled us to God. Since his death and resurrection we've made excuses for putting barriers back up. Often we raise them in his name, to defend human doctrines we believe to be holy. Lord, forgive us again. And again. And again.

Learning

Psalm 111

Wisdom is a precious commodity. As the saying goes, we are too soon old and too late smart. Experience has a way of teaching us. Most of us learn to make judgments about future consequences based on past events. In our late teens and early twenties, we may not trust the experiences of others. We insist on making our own mistakes (mostly because we're certain we're not making mistakes at the time). Some lessons are more painful than others. As time goes by, we sometimes take the shortcut of learning from the experiences of others.

The Bible recommends the shortcut method. It points out the foolishness of ignoring the counsel of your parents and elders. The Bible also teaches us to rely on our Creator. It makes sense that the One who created us in the first place knows what's best for us. Our gracious and compassionate God can be the first one to whom we turn for guidance.

Wisdom begins with the fear of this Lord. Glorious, majestic, gracious, compassionate, faithful, just, and trustworthy add up to holy and awesome. Awe is a better description than fear. Fear of the Lord has more to do with wonder and reverence than dread and dismay. Reverent obedience to the commands of God is true wisdom. The Ten Commandments are not arbitrary restrictions on life, but the heart of an operator's manual. The laws of God are essential elements of the blueprint for a wise and successful life. A life lived without regard for God is full of trouble. A life lived in awe of the Lord is filled with wonder, joy, purpose. Which would you rather have today: an awful day or an awe-full day?

Making beds

Isaiah 57:6-8

"You made your bed, now lie in it, " is an old saying that remains current. Our deeds catch up with us. They form the context, the bed, of our lives. We are always building our futures, making our beds. Of course, many events are out of our control. We do not choose the family into which we are born, nor the era of our birth, but on the whole we choose our work, our friends, and our church. We choose how to relate to the human circle around us and we choose how we will relate to God. It is these close relations in which we "bed down" for many years.

Eating crackers in bed is a notorious no-no. Those tasty saltines may assuage late evening rumblings of the stomach, but those crumbs make for a restless, uncomfortable night. Another bad practice is sleeping on a run-down mattress and box spring. A bed should support the sleeper's body, especially his or her back. A night on a rotten bed leads to a rotten next day. We can endure it for a time, but eventually we come to our senses and buy a new mattress.

In a similar vein, there are better and worse ways of making our spiritual beds. If we neglect the religious part of our life, we will suffer the consequences. We can join with hedonists in pursuit of immediate pleasure and "high times" until we are exhausted. Or we can spend time in prayer and Bible study until we gain sight of God's will for us. There are many ways to make a spiritual bed that can offer rest, renewal, and comfort. How did you sleep last night?

Outcast

Luke 17:11-19

The life of first century lepers was precarious. They had to cover their mouths, keep their distance, and cry "Unclean!" in the presence of others. Fear of catching the dreaded disease made them complete outcasts. Forced to live outside the city or camp, they were dependent on the charity of others.

Jews treated Samaritans almost like lepers. The idea of sharing cooking utensils or any personal item with them was repulsive. "Good Jews" wouldn't set foot in Samaria if they could avoid it. The name "Good Samaritan," by which we know the story in Luke 10 was a contradiction in terms.

Jesus tended to ignore the social protocol of his day. He ate with whom he chose. He touched and healed whomever he wanted. He walked through Samaria instead of detouring around it. He used the ancient enmity between Jew and Samaritan to highlight the inclusive nature of the kingdom of God. The Good Samaritan parable turns Jewish expectations on their heads. In today's story of the lepers, the one who returns to say thank you is a Samaritan. He shows better manners and truer gratitude than the rest. In both cases it is the outsider, the foreigner, who is more in touch with God than the good "church people."

But that was during Jesus' time; this is the 1990s. Now it's the church folk who are on Jesus' side. Is that so? Who are the lepers of today who cry for mercy from the roadside: People with AIDS? Homeless persons? Single "welfare mothers?" What areas of our cities do we detour around out of fear and loathing? Are we willing to touch those whom Jesus would touch?

Enemies

Psalm 3

Someone once made the comment that they had hard time hearing Jesus' command to love our enemies because they really couldn't identify enemies in their life. They could readily identify people who irritated them and got on their nerves, but not people they considered to be enemies.

Perhaps as you read this, you find yourself envying that person, because your enemies are all too real. Perhaps a jealous co-worker has been sabotaging your projects. Or someone is spreading false stories behind your back, damaging your reputation. Whatever the cause or the case, you can echo the words of the psalmist when he declares, "How many are my foes!" Haven't we all felt like that at some time? It seems as if no matter which way you turn, there is a battle to be fought.

In truth, we all have our enemies. Some of them may be easily identified, easily recognized. Others are more subtle. Your enemy may come in the form of an unjust system that would deny you opportunities to develop and use your God-given gifts. It may be persons who, while they do not actively oppose you, demean your intelligence or abilities, and serve as a roadblock to whatever you would accomplish. There are enemies who delight in punching holes in our dreams. And, like the comic strip character Pogo, we do well to recognize that sometimes we are our own enemies.

But we do well to also remember that we are not alone. No matter how isolated we may feel under fire, we are not alone. There is God, and God is for us. And like the psalmist, we may abandon ourselves to the peace of sleep, sustained in the knowledge that God will not abandon us.

Transition

2 Timothy 4:4-8

A minister leaves a church after years of service. A teacher retires after years in the classroom. A business executive moves to another company.

Times of transition are times for evaluation. What did I accomplish? What do I leave behind that is of value? What difference has this time made? A minister may point to new buildings or increases in membership, the teacher to students who have gone on to distinguish themselves. The executive sees increased productivity or a more profitable bottom line.

What did I accomplish? It's a question that all of us ask sooner or later, to one degree or another. For some, the question comes as they face the end of their lives.

Such was the situation that Paul faced. He could see the broad outlines of his own death on the near horizon. The time of his ministry was drawing to a close. He was passing the torch on to Timothy.

We would have understood if Paul had waxed eloquent or grown nostalgic over his accomplishments in ministry. After all, he had a distinguished career to review. Who could blame Paul if he added up the number of churches he had established, or reviewed the importance of his role in opening up missionary efforts to the Gentiles? (Paul wasn't shy about discussing his achievements at other times in his life!) But now, facing the end of that life, he does none of that. He simply says, "I have kept the faith."

There are many yardsticks by which to measure the success of an individual or a church. Paul knew the only measurement that ultimately mattered. "I have kept the faith." It was the most he could say. It is the most we can do.

Sinner she was

Luke 7:36-50

Her reputation had unraveled,
picked apart by self-righteous hands,
weavers in reverse.
Her pride faded like empty colors
until all she knew of herself
was what others said.
She was evil; she was wrong.
Sinner she was, branded and worthless.
Sinner she was, dirty and useless.
But there came a man with love in his eye
and forgiveness on his lips.
Sinner she was, but forgiven she was.
And her life came back to her.
They didn't understand,
these that never knew the weight of shame,
that never danced with despair.
So perfect, they'd never been healed.
So perfect, they'd never been forgiven.
So perfect, they'd never needed anything
or anyone more than themselves.
But she knew what it was to need,
and her broken heart cried glad tears.
He was her Lord; he was the Christ.

What Doozers do

Haggai 2:1-9

❧ "Fraggle Rock" is a children's television program which features furry, fun-loving creatures known as Fraggles who love to swim and play all day long. Yet they encounter problems like we do.

The world isn't just populated with Fraggles. There are the Gorks, giants whose primary ambitions are to grow vegetables and catch Fraggles. Then there are the Doozers, six-inch, green Pillsbury dough people who are constantly building things out of the Gorks' vegetables for the Fraggles to eat. The Doozers' primary ambition is to build these vegetable towers. Yet they encounter problems like we do.

It seems that Cotter Pin Doozer decided she didn't want to put on her hard hat and build. And so she set out to become a Fraggle. Everything was going nicely. She enjoyed singing the Fraggle Song with the Whistling Cave Hum Bugs. She loved racing to the swimming pool with Red Fraggle. But when Red told her that all Fraggles had to swim, she replied, "Doozers don't swim!" It was then that Cotter Pin realized she was a Doozer, not your typical Doozer, but a Doozer nonetheless; a Doozer encountering problems like we do.

Returning home, Cotter Pin discovered that not all Doozers build. Some must be architects for the builders. And so Cotter Pin Doozer freely chose to become an architect and loved it in spite of encountering problems.

Hibernation

2 Corinthians 5:16-21

A test was given at little Emma's school, asking the question: "Upon what do hibernating animals exist during the winter?" After much thought and deliberation, Emma wrote: "On the hope of coming spring."

How many of us spiritually hibernating creatures rely on the hope of a miraculous change to somehow stir us from our insensitive slumber? As pilgrims struggling to jump over the hurdles that life sets before us, we come to the realization one day that life with Christ is an endless hope, without Christ a hopeless end. The day we claim the promise of God in Christ, we are reconciled. How joyous our hearts, how light our souls when our hope is reality: we have become new!

Yet how heavy our hearts and sad our souls can become when we cease our reconciled living, crawl into a cave of life, and hibernate again. Who can revive us when our hearts beat occasionally and our souls sleep, insensitive to the need for spiritual growth in our own lives and spiritual change in the lives of untold others? The world's lullaby is seductive and appealing. We easily fall for the "Everybody else is hibernating" ploy. Who can revive us?

"So if anyone is in Christ, there is a new creation." Jesus Christ can stir us from our deepest spiritual hibernation. God is the one who transforms impossibilities into realities. With God there are no dead-end streets, only crossroads!

Perhaps our question could be better phrased: "Upon what do hibernating persons exist during the winter of their souls?" In faith, we can respond: "God in Christ reconciling us."

Not knowing

Genesis 12:1-3

Most of the time when I travel by car, I'm going to a place that I've visited before. Whether I'm driving to the mountains or the beach, the roads are familiar. That kind of travel is easy; I know the landmarks, the easy-to-miss turns. I know where I'm going and how long it will take me to get there.

Going somewhere new is a different story. I have to keep looking at the map, not knowing exactly how long before I have to make a turn. I don't know how long it'll take for me to get there, or what my destination will look like when I arrive.

But that's the kind of travel faith asks of us. We go even though we're not sure of the destination nor what the journey will ask of us. We don't know if the next bend in the road will bring us an oasis or a desert. All we are promised is that God goes with us.

Traveling familiar roads is easy. But God asks us to go beyond the familiar and comfortable. Sometimes we are called to leave behind a vision of this world that is too provincial. Sometimes it is a calling to leave behind distorted images of ourselves that deny both our giftedness and our brokenness. Sometimes we are even called to leave behind a faith that has grown too small and timid.

"Go," God said to Abraham, and to each one of us. Like Abraham, we don't know what this journey brings. Like Paul, we don't know what we shall yet be. But the people of God are people of the journey.

Reflect this day on your own journey of faith, even as you listen again for God's call.

Joining up

Matthew 8:18-22

Any good salesperson will tell you that you have to strike while the iron is hot. Take advantage of that moment of interest, that glimmer of possibility.

Such was the moment that Jesus faced. Having healed Peter's mother-in-law of a fever, he was now faced with many others who had been brought to him to be healed. It was a golden opportunity to sign up new disciples. Enthusiasm ran high. All he needed was a registration table at the door, and enough enrollment slips.

But Jesus misses the moment. He doesn't just miss the moment, he deliberately passes it up. Seeing the crowds, he tells the disciples to go with him to the other side of the lake. Some of the people follow him even there, eager to join up.

One man volunteers to follow Jesus, unaware that to walk the way with this man means to wind up at a cross. Another wants to follow as soon as he has exercised his sacred obligation to bury his father. But following Jesus takes precedence over both religious rules and family ties.

Jesus' responses are hardly the stuff of a slick ad campaign. They wouldn't look appealing in a newspaper ad or sound inviting in a thirty-second commercial. But then again, that wasn't Jesus' concern.

He didn't want disciples who followed him because he performed a miracle or two. He didn't want disciples who were there because they had gotten caught up in the enthusiasm of a crowd. He didn't want disciples who wanted to follow when it was convenient for them. He wanted people who would come and die.

Here is no easy-to-join club with watered-down demands. Here is a Lord asking for our lives.

Injustice

Psalm 94:12-22

Sometimes, O Lord, I know I sound like a five-year-old, standing with her lip out and stamping her foot. I'm grown and I ought to know better, but sometimes I still want to crawl up into your lap and whine, "Life's not fair."

In my grown-up head, I know that's the way things work. But sometimes it seems more unfair than others. I find it hard to watch the people who play by the rules and never get anywhere. They live decent lives; they try to follow you. They are faithful and good, but they always wind up on the short end of the stick. Sometimes I just have to ask, "Why?"

And sometimes, O God, it's hard to watch the people who do prosper. Sometimes it's the ones who always take the shortcuts. People who don't care about you and don't care about their brothers and sisters. They care only for themselves, but they get ahead in life. It's just not fair, this life.

I don't know if it'd be easier to have the answers to my questions, but I guess I never will. Remind me, O God, when the winds of life blow too harshly, you are my refuge. When I skin my knees and my soul on the unfairness of it all, you are my strength. When I'm discouraged by the triumph of the darkness, you are my light.

I don't understand the twists and turns of life. But I know that you understand my questions, for you have suffered at the hands of injustice. You have the scars to prove it. Help me remember that injustice doesn't have the last word. That word belongs to you.

Steadfastness

Jeremiah 31:1-6

In the text it is obvious that, in spite of our stubborn resistance, God wills a continuing relationship with us. If you were God, would you yearn for a relationship with a people who take you for granted, go against your best desires for them and their welfare, or ignore you completely? If we were God, we probably would be tempted to move on, leaving humankind to its own devices. However, the whole biblical witness reveals that God envisions a renewed relationship and works with persistence and resolve to bring it about.

Why is this the case? It is only because God loves us with a love that will not quit, a steadfast, enduring love that does not depend on the present circumstances.

There is a little dog named "Patches" who lives at our house. In all honesty, he isn't worth much. He cowers under the buffet in the kitchen when we have guests. He won't roll over, sit, or even obey the most elementary command. However, there is a little nine-year old girl who lives at our house who faithfully feeds and cares for Patches. Because of this little girl's great love for him, Patches is a most esteemed and loved member of our family.

Are we any different from that little dog? For some reason known only to God, the creator, redeemer and sustainer of all history has chosen to love you and me. That love gives us great worth.

There is nothing within our power to create or earn God's love for us. The only thing we can do is accept that love and allow it to do its good work in our lives. That is good news for today and every day!

45

College prayer

Luke 16:19-31

Like Peter, sometimes I get carried away, Lord.
Command of me some great and heroic sacrifice.
Let me be put in the midst of a grand and awful hour of
decision,
Let me do something big and wonderful and awe-inspiring.

Forgive me, Lord,
for sometimes I get so carried away
in my dreams of grandeur
that I forget
Your kingdom comes in ordinary moments
common hours
simple, small acts.

Help me be faithful, O God, in the little things
to listen with love
even if I've heard the story before,
to offer a hug and give a smile
to someone running low on both,
a dinner
a night of watching someone else's children
a letter written or a card sent.

It doesn't seem like much, God.
I'd rather cure cancer or achieve world peace.
But remind me that in Your kingdom,
this kingdom of sparrows and wildflowers and mustard seeds,

to be faithful in little is to be faithful in much.

God's love

Psalm 107:33-43

Psalm 107 celebrates the faithfulness of God's love by recounting examples of God's deliverance. The hungry and the imprisoned, the sick and those in danger upon the sea, all have been saved through the gracious love of God. God provides for them water in the midst of a desert and a city in which to dwell.

The love of God is never an abstract thing for the psalmist, but is always fleshed out in the nitty-gritty of life. The matter of their faith was always bound up with matters of their lives.

This psalm, like many others, calls us to give thanks for "the steadfast love of the Lord." This is the love that won't give up on us, even when we've given up on God and ourselves. When the icy hand of fear holds us in its grasp, this love wraps us up like the warmth of a family quilt. In the midst of our darkness, this love punches a hole of light like a star in the night sky. This love heals us, so that we laugh, even when we thought we could never smile again. We sing, even after we thought our songs had all been taken from us.

The psalmist tells us the stories of many who have been touched and saved by the steadfast love of God. The saints from the ages would weave their testimony into this tapestry as well.

What's your story? Take time this day to reflect upon your life, upon those times when you most felt the love of God and give thanks. If this is one of those dark times, remember God's love that once was present in your life, and give thanks. For it will be true for you again.

Loss

Joel 2:25-27

Sitting in the Thanksgiving service, he felt more grief than thanksgiving. Deep in a loss that was both fresh and devastating, he wondered why he had even come to church that night. He certainly didn't feel like singing great hymns of praise.

Then the minister stood to read the Old Testament text, this very passage from the book of Joel. As the prophet's words rang out through the sanctuary, he felt as if he was being given something to hold on to. It was a word that wrapped his tender wounds with hope and promise. Suddenly he knew exactly why he was there. If there was not yet thanksgiving in his heart, there could be the hope of it.

"I will repay the years that the locusts have eaten." Some of us have lost days and years through tough choices and wrong turns. Like Israel, we turned from God's way and found only disaster. For others, the days are lost in grief or illness. Some have lost the years of their childhood due to abuse. Some have seen their dreams slip away.

In a real sense, what is gone cannot be recaptured. The loved one who has died can never be replaced. Our lives cannot be lived all over again. Yet the word of the Lord comes, and it is a word of hope. There is yet more to come.

Once again, God says to Israel, the rains will come and the crops will flourish and the devouring locusts will depart. Once again, God says to us, your life will be abundant.

The day of disaster doesn't last forever; neither does the night of grief. I will look on you with love, God says, and will fill your life with my grace.

Choose life

Deut. 30:11-20

This passage of scripture is part of Moses' final sermon to the Israelites before they go into the Promised Land. Like any good spiritual leader, Moses knows human nature. Under stress of what is new, strange and unknown, we tend to revert to the "not me" stance in order to avoid responsibility.

Like the Israelites, fear of the unknown can make us deny life and the promise of the future. We want someone else to make the final decision and be responsible for what happens.

Scripture's assurance is that the word is near to us, by its witness and the life of Jesus and other Christians. God's word is in our own hearts. We don't have to wait to choose life and claim God's promises to us.

But we do have to choose between life and death, blessings and curses. God's promise is not without challenge. Since Eden, we are individually responsible for choosing what God offers. It is possible to live out our lives with hearts turned away from this challenge; other gods will entice us from the God of deliverance.

Moses gives the Israelites, and us, a short, poetic rule for those times when we stand facing the unknown, wondering whether we dare claim God's promises.

> Choose life.
> Love the Lord your God.
> Obey the Lord your God.
> Hold fast to God.
> What is the unknown for you today? What is your sense of God's promise for you? What is the challenge you face?

Imposter syndrome

Deuteronomy 7:6-11

Some successful people suffer from what has been called "the imposter syndrome." They may be successful in business, or successful in the cultivation of many friendships, but they don't feel deserving of their success. If they only knew what I was really like, they reason to themselves, they wouldn't think I was so great. I'm not really qualified. I feel like an imposter.

Why did you choose me? Why did you choose me for your kickball team, or for the new promotion, or to head up the stewardship drive at the church? Those doing the choosing may speak of gifts. But those being chosen worry about measuring up, about not being "found out."

Why did you choose me? God answered the question for Israel. I didn't choose you because you were the greatest nation on earth, or the biggest, God tells them. I chose you because I love you. That's all. That's it.

And so it is for us. God did not choose us to be sons and daughters because we measured up to some divine standard. God didn't choose us because our carefully compiled list of achievements was so impressive. We don't have to worry about being "found out" and kicked out, because God already knows us. The real us. God knows our greatest achievements and our most painful failures, and all the times we didn't even try. And all of that doesn't matter.

We don't have to prove ourselves deserving. We don't have to hide our imperfections. We don't have to be anybody other than the unique people God created us to be.

God choose us because God loves us. We cannot earn it and we cannot make it go away. God loves us. That's it. That's all. And that is grace.

Commandments

Exodus 20:1-20

For some people, the Decalogue (Ten Commandments) is baffling and completely overwhelming. For others, these commandments of God are a guide and directive for living life with the best of relationships.

We cannot break the Ten Commandments any more than we can break the law of gravity. However, these words of God will break us if we live contrary to their teachings as we relate to God and humankind.

You may think of the Ten Commandments like the old man who wrote the Lord's prayer on a brown paper bag and hung it on his wall. When he went to bed he lay down, looked up at the prayer and said, "Lord, them's my sentiments!"

You may chuckle at that, but in seriousness that's the way some of us view our relationships with God and each other. That kind of action just doesn't get it, does it?

We are called as the followers of faith to put these commandments of God into daily practice as we relate to God and as we develop our relationships with those around us. That's the hard part.

Jesus beautifully summarized these ten guidelines into a familiar teaching: "Love the Lord your God with all your heart, and with all your soul, and with all your mind . . . You shall love your neighbor as yourself" (Matt 22:37, 39). It is how we follow Christ in our relationship to God and in our encounters with each other that really counts, anyway!

Lord, give me strength today to develop a new relationship with you. Teach me to be more open to developing my Christian character around my associates. Amen.

Finding help

Jeremiah 33:1-9

When the chips are down, have you ever tried to "outdo" God? Sure you have! Business may be lousy, but by your own strength and business acumen, you try to get it on the right track. A family member or close friend may be dying of cancer or AIDS, and you turn to the very best medical facility you know. A teenager may be driving you insane. You scream and yell and threaten and may even revert to assertive discipline. Many times we exhaust our own resources and then turn to God.

Jeremiah was shut in the guard house. How demeaning and threatening for the prophet of God! In the middle of that depression, God said, "Call to me and I will answer you, and will tell you great and hidden things which you have not known" (v. 3). How refreshing! In the middle of his trouble, God reassured Jeremiah. It's like being in the middle of some experience from which you think there is no escape and someone says, "There is help. Let's find it."

We need that kind of voice and reinforcement on our journey of faith. The good news of grace is found in the One who forged the path and says, "This is the way; walk ye in it." When we forget those things that seem to be utmost in our lives and walk in God's way, we know that we cannot "outdo" God.

Grace-gifts

Genesis 50:15-21

Honest forgiveness is one of the hardest tasks to which God calls us. How do you forgive the thief or murderer when that robbery or death affects your life? How do you forgive one who slanders you or wrongs you when your character is on the firing line? That kind of forgiveness is not an easy task, but it is one to which we are called. Jesus set forth the supreme example by uttering a prayer of forgiveness on his cross: "Father, forgive them for they know not what they do."

Some years ago there was a popular song based on a mountain legend about a young man whose life went sour. Despite his being reared in a devout and religious home, he ended up in prison for taking a man's life. When his sentence was almost completed, he wrote a letter to his mother, begging her forgiveness for all of the unhappiness he had caused. He asked her that if she could find it in her heart to forgive him, to tie a white cloth on the old oak tree in front of their house as her sign of forgiveness. As the bus made the familiar turn in the bend of the road and his home came into view, the sight was breathtaking. Not only the old oak tree, but the house and the barn and the fences were covered with strips of white cloth.

So it is with God. We ask for little, and we receive a lot of grace-gifts. We ask God to forgive us as sinners, and God makes us saints.

God, I want to forgive all my enemies. I really do! But somehow I just can't quite do that. Teach me how, through Jesus Christ, to really learn how to forgive. Amen.

Judging

Romans 14:13-19

It's so easy to criticize others, isn't it? All too often we become too judgmental because someone doesn't handle the situation as we would, or doesn't discipline a child as we would discipline ours, or become involved in a civic project to which we think he or she should have given valuable time. We revert to criticism which gives over to a judgmental nature.

The old Native American proverb speaks a very loud truth: "Don't judge until you have walked a mile in another person's moccasins!" That kind of understanding is called "empathy." When you show empathy, you try to project yourself into some other person's shoes. You try your best to see exactly how things seem to him or her. Even after that, you may not agree, but you are in a better position to sincerely say, "I really don't like your idea, but let's try to work something out."

That is no magical formula to overcoming criticism, but it does help us to be more acceptable to God, to ourselves, and to each other. It will help us to be less disagreeable, less judgmental, and less critical. You really have nothing to lose by "walking in someone's shoes." In fact, it may make your feet hurt so bad that you have a new understanding of what it is to have a Christ-like attitude.

O God, I remember that I too will stand before the judgment seat of Christ and will give an account of my dealings and attitudes with my fellows. Please don't judge me the way I am prone to judge others! Amen.

Bringing God close

Exodus 32:1-14

Only human beings can make vows. And only human beings can break them. Our text for consideration is about how quickly the people of Israel broke the covenant with God. They did so by making a golden bull and worshipping it. Then Moses prayed for his people.

But first, why did they do it? Perhaps it was fear. Moses had been up on Sinai for a long time and they were afraid they had lost their leader. They faced the unknown without the one who had led them out of Egyptian slavery. But even more significant, they felt that God was far off.

So the need was for a god who was close, one they could touch and who would go with them on their difficult journey. Thus they fashioned an idol, toasted it, danced around it, and offered sacrifices to it.

Makes sense to me, but the writer believed it was wrong because it was disobeying God (v. 8). He has a point, because putting our way over God's is never right. But more importantly, they broke a promise. This is a bad habit to get into. It has hurt more marriages, broken more homes, destroyed more human relationships than anything I can think of. Making and keeping our promises is an important part of life.

This molten image put Moses in a bind. He cared for both his people and his God. He shrewdly reminded God of the promises God had made to Israel. And God was so impressed with Moses' compassion that God was moved from anger to pity.

Prayer changes things. Isn't that it? And when prayer can't change things, perhaps it can change us. Moses prayed for his people because he cared for them but he also cared about God. Would that more of our prayers moved the Almighty like Moses' did.

55

Special interests

Isaiah 64:1-9

I'm convinced that the curse of gridlock in our government lies at the feet of special interests. Each group lobbying for its own financial concerns makes it practically impossible for our kind of government to work efficiently. Indeed, President Bill Clinton has his work cut out for him.

John D. W. Watts points out in *The Word Biblical Commentary* that our text from Isaiah's day shows us that special interests are nothing new. They've been around a long time. The verses before us make up part of a sermon/prayer, which is preempted by those with special sectarian concerns. Some pray exclusively for Jerusalem; others for all twelve tribes. Some are concerned only for the Temple. There are activists who demand a return to political power and military might that is guaranteed to win the respect of other nations.

The problem with special interest prayer is that it ignores God's work in other areas. It thinks only in terms of what God did once, a long time ago, and longs for a return to that kind of action as they imagine it. No wonder they lament and confess their sins!

Then the petitioner takes a more universal spirit and prays for all the people, by addressing the Lord as "our Father," he gets more inclusive and intimate. This assumes that they are all in this together. That God is Israel's maker. He drives the image home with the model of the potter and clay. Because the Israelites are the work of the hands of God, they might expect God to be concerned about their condition.

This leads to the conviction that dealt a severe blow to special interest prayer: "We are your people." Now that's more like it.

Nothing to lose

Philippians 1:21-27

Americans have come to expect success. We are accustomed to winning. But we need a theology of loss. We'd better learn how to lose. For if we live long enough and love somebody enough, sooner or later, lose we will. Then what?

"Freedom's just another word for nothing left to lose . . . " wrote Kristofferson. When we have nothing to lose, it's sort of liberating, I suppose he's saying. And I feel somewhat for those who have a lot; they have a lot to lose.

In our text, Paul finds himself in a "can't lose" situation. Indeed, he struggles with life and offers this philosophy: "For me to live in Christ and to die [lose] is gain." Paul's outlook had to do with winning and losing. Whether he lived or died, he could not lose. Sounds like the lyrics of "Bobby McGee," doesn't it?

Paul was in a win/win situation. Life was complex enough for Paul for him to be "torn between the two," but "whether he remains or leaves this world," he cannot lose! Can you imagine that?

We should be able to imagine that because we have the same source of hope as Paul: prayer, God's presence, and a positive philosophy of life. Whether he went to heaven or stayed on earth, Paul believed he couldn't lose because Christ was first in his life. To me, he said, "To live is Christ!"

What do you say? For me to live is _____. Pray that you will be able to "seek first God's kingdom and righteousness, and all these things will be added unto you" (Matt 6:33). Anybody who can do that cannot lose.

Trust

Psalm 25:1-10

Psychologist Erik Erikson's theory of human development describes eight tasks people face. The first one is "basic trust." This is a foundational. If a child at an early age does not develop the capacity to trust, to have confidence in the trustworthiness of those who provide care and to feel secure in surrounding love, development through succeeding stages will likely be retarded. In some cases wholeness may never be achieved.

Just as trust is necessary for healthy emotional development, so it is basic to healthy spiritual development. The prayer of the psalmist begins with an affirmation of trust—"In you, my God, I trust." With trust undergirding his life, he was able to deal with enemies, know that God's forgiveness can be depended on and look with confidence to the future.

Trust is that part of the faith experience that enables us to put our lives into God's hands, betting our lives on the trustworthiness of God.

All three synoptic Gospels tell the lovely story of Jesus blessing the children. The passage closes with Jesus' statement: "Remember this! Whoever does not receive the kingdom of God like a child will never enter it" (TEV). What did Jesus mean? Humility, innocence, and obedience have been suggested as characteristics that Jesus may have had in mind. However, every parent knows that children do not always display such qualities. Children are, however, dependent. Their whole life is built in trust. When crises come they freely turn to others for help. It is not childishness or immaturity that Jesus sees as a requirement for entering the kingdom, but an attitude of simple trust. Perhaps a kind of "second childhood" is required of us if we would enter the kingdom of God.

Futility

Ecclesiastes 3:13-18

Ecclesiastes was not readily accepted into the Old Testament canon but it has always been a favorite reading experience of mine. True, the outlook of the preacher/philosopher who wrote it is pessimistic and gloomy. True, the theme that runs through the book is that everything is vanity since the end of all, good or evil, rich or poor, wise or foolish, is a return to dust.

Still, he is honest about his own conclusions and he speaks to many today. How many have sought satisfaction through wisdom, wealth, work or pleasure only to realize the futility of their efforts? How many take seriously the suffering, injustice and hopelessness in our world and rage against their own helplessness and a God who seems not to care? How many believe in God, as this writer unquestionably does, but find God remote and silent in their search for answers?

The response of the writer of Ecclesiastes to all is this: accept joy, suffering and injustice as part of life. Eat, drink, enjoy what you have for it is from God. There are few answers to our many questions so forget them and get all the joy you can from each day. What will be, will be.

We may see something of ourselves mirrored in these words, but as Christians we know there is meaning and purpose in life. We worship a God who is gracious, merciful, forgiving and loving and who does care about injustice and suffering. We believe that life is more than a journey from dust back to dust. Many of the questions we ask are the same ones this writer asks.

Sins of the parents

Ezekiel 18:1-4, 25-32

❦ "The parents ate the sour grapes and the children got the sour taste" (TEV) was a proverb well known by the people. Jeremiah quoted it (31:29) but said the day had already come. God will judge each one and hold none responsible for the sins of others.

That the sins of the parents and of society are indeed visited upon those who follow can hardly be denied. The addicted baby of a crack-dependent mother and the tormented teenager sexually abused by a parent are but two examples that could be multiplied endlessly. A national debt that is now so large most of us cannot comprehend it and an environment that is increasingly being destroyed are but two of the evils the present generation will pass on to the next. It may be for good or for evil, it may be blessing or curse.

We do suffer from the sins of others as they suffer from ours, and there is no way to separate ourselves from the past. Ezekiel surely knew this, but he insists there is justice in the end. God knows us personally and knows where the blame justly belongs. We will not be held responsible for the sins of others. We will not even be held responsible for our own past sins if they are forgiven.

How easy it is to place the blame elsewhere for the evil we do. But no matter how effectively we are able to explain away our weaknesses and wrongdoing, in the end God, who knows us better than we know ourselves, will judge us with both love and righteousness.

Prisoner

Ephesians 3:1-12

I have never wanted to be a prisoner. Stories I've heard about life behind bars terrify me. The mental, emotional, physical, and spiritual anguish of prison life must be incredibly painful.

But there are also other kinds of prisons I have heard about that also terrify me. In listening to people tell their stories, I have heard them tell of being a prisoner to alcohol, drugs, food, sex, relationships, gambling, and even religion. Such stories tell of mental, emotional, physical and spiritual anguish every bit as painful as life behind bars.

Rigorous honesty requires that I stop focusing on the stories of others for a moment and try to get in touch with my own story of prison life. With regularity I can become prisoner to fear, pride or self-doubt. Such feelings restrict my freedom to live abundantly. When I begin to live in light of those destructive feelings, I am just as much a prisoner as any felon in the land.

In Ephesians 3, the Apostle Paul offers an interesting twist to the idea of being a prisoner. Paul says that he is a prisoner of Jesus Christ. What a wonderful image! What a frightening image!

To be a prisoner of Jesus Christ means that I have turned myself over to Jesus. It means that I am under Christ's control. No longer am I imprisoned by self-destructive attitudes and behaviors, but instead am controlled by love, joy, peace, patience, kindness, goodness, faithfulness, and gentleness.

O God, give me the wisdom and the will to say "no" to the option of being a prisoner to society or to the self, and to say "yes" to being a prisoner of your love.

Wise men

Matthew 2:1-12

What does it take to be a wise man? I first asked that question when I was in the fourth grade. The two fourth grade classes in our school were preparing for the annual Christmas play.

When our music teacher revealed who had been chosen to play the various parts, I was crushed to find out I was not one of the three wise men. Herman, Donald and Greg got the parts. I could understand Herman and Donald getting to be wise men because they were much taller than the rest of us. All the wise people I knew then were taller than I was, so that made sense. But why Greg? He was shorter than I was, and he even wore glasses.

That was it! Suddenly I realized why these three had been chosen. They all wore glasses! That revelation helped me more graciously accept my role as a mindless and speechless shepherd. Yet when the big night came, I was crushed to see these three wise men make their grand entrance carrying gold, frankincense and myrrh, but wearing no glasses.

To this day, I can't sing or hear "We Three Kings" without feeling a few pangs of jealousy.

One of my current working definitions of wisdom is: Attentiveness to all of the ways God is revealing God's self to us. I was close back there in the fourth grade with that notion of glasses. Wisdom does have to do with our seeing God more clearly.

On this Epiphany, 1994, we celebrate the awareness that God has come for persons in every corner of the world, as well as to every corner of our personal world.

May God grant to each of us the wisdom and vision to see the self-revelation of God.

Strength and peace

Psalm 29

Today the psalmist reminds me of one of the great truths of our faith—that God gives me what I most desperately need.

When David wrote this psalm, he was reflecting specifically on how God blesses us with strength and with peace.

I grew up in a city that was located near a military base. Soldiers were constantly being trained to go to war. That meant that at any time during the day or night we might hear the distant rumble of huge artillery rounds going off as these soldiers were training for combat.

I grew up at a time when the Cold War was at its peak. Politicians and military experts preached strength to the American people. Their message was that our nation must build an enormous military power in order to assure our national security, and hence, our peace.

In the last verse of Psalm 29, David is speaking of God's strength and God's peace. Even as a young man, David knew that the only kind of peace that really mattered could not be obtained by military might. When David was preparing to go to battle against the Philistine giant, his friends tried to dress him in the finest armor of that day. But the armor neither fit his body nor his faith. David chose not to trust the finest armor of his day, and chose to trust in the strength of God.

Too often my armor can isolate me from my greatest Strength. God does indeed bless me with God's strength and peace, but I must first take off all my armor and relax into God's strong and peaceful arms.

Takes all kinds

Mark 1:4-11

✤ "It takes all kinds." I can't find that quote anywhere in the Bible, but I'm sure that words to that effect must surely have fallen from the lips of our Lord at some time or another. Perhaps someday Indiana Jones will unearth the long-lost Gospel of Andrew, and right there in red letters will be those words as spoken by Jesus himself.

I would guess that the context for those words would be a conversation between Jesus and some honest inquirer. After several days of following Jesus and his disciples around Galilee, they would catch Jesus away from his disciples and ask a question that had been nagging them for a few days. They would point out to Jesus that he had a rather strange mixture of people following him. Maybe they would mention certain personality quirks they had observed in some of Jesus' followers. They might even use the Greek word for "bizarre" as they pointed to some of Jesus' followers.

When they had finished with their assessment of his followers, I think the writer would remember that Jesus looked at them, smiled, and said, "Well, you know, it takes all kinds."

I need to hear that important truth because I know when I look at some of the biblical characters who followed Jesus, I shake my head and wonder what he saw in them.

One of the gospel characters who has annoyed me most is John the baptizer. His wardrobe, his diet, and his televangelistic zeal bother me. Today's incarnations of John the baptizer bother me even more.

Yet, Mark 1 shows me that John had a prominent role in the life and ministry of Christ. He was not only acceptable to God, but also necessary.

Today, I will work to accept all of Jesus' followers because "it takes all kinds."

Intention

Psalm 67

Several months ago I heard a pastor give a brief lesson on how to pray in public. He said that this type of prayer should include six parts: an address of God, a second address, a petition or request, an intention or reasoning why the request should be granted, and ascription (signing off), and finally the listeners' "amen," provided that they support the prayer, of course.

The pastor continued, saying that the element of public prayer we almost always exclude is the intention. I believe this is the case with our private prayers as well. Our tendency to greet God, make our request, and then sign off ignoring any responsibility that might be ours to own. How readily we say, "give me," and how slowly we continue with, "so that I might offer this."

Did you notice that the psalmist did include an intention in this prayer? God's blessing is requested so that God's "way may be known upon earth," so that God's "saving power (may be known) among all nations."

All of us long and ask for God's graciousness and blessing. All of us pray for God's grace to shine upon us. This is good,but why do we do it? Do we ask of God that our lives may become easier, so that we might live in warm, cozy comfort? Or do we ask of God so that we might be empowered to serve, so that we might be enabled to share God's "way upon earth," God's "saving power among all nations," God's love with all whom we encounter?

Maybe for a moment we should back up and slip into the shoes of that early disciple who said, "Lord, teach us to pray . . . " Then I think God's face can shine.

Divorce

Mark 10:1-12

⤳ "Is it unlawful for a man to divorce his wife?" (v. 2b)

Divorce has always been a difficult subject. That's why these Pharisees hoped to embarrass or trap Jesus with their question. Earlier, Jesus had said to the people, "Be perfect . . . " (Matt 5:48). Love everyone in all relationships the way that God loves you, Christ taught. But no one can live up to that except Christ, so what can we do?

Though we know we will fail God and will fail one another, perfection in love still remains our goal. The Pharisees said Moses had let them divorce. Jesus immediately reminded them of the goal, God's original plan: "From the beginning of creation" God created us as persons who may become, in love, as one.

Keep this standard of a perfect bond of love before you, Christ seems to say. Take marriage seriously and responsibly. Live with one another in all relationships sharing the bonds of love God makes possible. And if we fail, when we fail, as husband or wife, as parent, as minister, friend, or neighbor, we still turn to God.

For with God, if not always from one another, we find grace and mercy and a door to forgiveness. Live daily with the goal of attaining perfect love. But live also in dialogue with a God who honors honest repentance with the promise of new beginning.

Violence

Psalm 77:1-15

Who among us has not shuddered at the knowledge of rampant crime and violence in our own communities? Our anxieties heighten and our spirits crash each time we hear the news or read in the paper that someone has been shot and killed.

The psalmist is speaking such a lament, for the concern that is expressed is not merely a personal one, but one for a whole community of people. God's face is hidden; whether or not God is really in control is being questioned.

The problems that we face today are varied and complex. The results of violence and inhumanity are only symptoms of deeper, more insidious social ailments. Questions that we raise as we watch and read about the destruction most definitely parallel those of the psalmist.

But what can we do? What will we do? The writer, desperate and hopeless, remembers. The psalmist remembers the deeds of God, the past experiences that have formed the core of faith. It seems that even in the present gloom, God's past righteousness brings enough hope that the writer is able to continue living.

When we assess the major dilemmas of our day, it is easy to become exasperated. Our frustration is real and corresponds with the world's hopelessness. The good word, nonetheless, is that God's deeds of the past can empower our hopes for the future. Our encouragement is not to give up our hope, or to give in to inactivity. The aspirations of the people of God are based on faith in the Almighty, not fear of the world's woes. God invites us to remember the miracles of the past and to help prepare for the mighty acts of the future.

Integrity

Daniel 6:1-5

The story of Daniel reminds us of many important lessons, but none greater than living a life that corresponds to our confessed values and beliefs. Even young children are aware when someone's talk does not match their walk. This is one of the most disillusioning things for people outside the church looking in. Many of us are left with poor impressions of "church people."

Daniel impresses his captors initially because he is perceived as an honest, reliable and trustworthy individual. Because of his lifestyle he is a leader beyond reproach.

This story is so powerful because Daniel exhibits integration of his values and his behavior. His faith does not find the only outlet in speaking rights and wrongs, or pointing the finger at others. He is an example of conversion; individual, personal, and comprehensive.

Because he is illustrative of a virtuous person, his detractors seek his downfall by raising questions concerning his loyalty to the king. We are left wondering what they will find that might show him to be questionable.

Integrity is something we strive for in our daily lives. Only a full and sincere synthesis of our personal faith beliefs with particular behaviors that exhibit the spirit of our faith can lead others to trust us and our message.

Maybe Daniel was the beginner of what we today refer to as "lifestyle evangelism." Maybe if we looked upon his life as another model for righteous living, we would see more outstanding leaders in our world than we sometimes believe there are. Maybe we might look in the mirror and see a potential leader waiting to live a life of integrity, and, therefore, a more sincere witness for Christ.

Choosing to move

Genesis 12:1-9

I know a man who is in the midst of a job transition. He is not merely transitioning, but is moving from a large, successful company into forming his own firm. As we talked about the change, I could sense excitement as well as anxiety, courage as well as fear. He has a dry sense of humor and uses this gift to cover his concern, but this day I could tell the depth of his struggle. He wanted to be sure of his choice, but he was not.

When reading this text, I am struck by the fact that Abram and Sara are so trusting in God's leadership. God says "Go," and off they go. And along the journey, they stop to worship and thank God for the promises offered and the future ahead. They seem so certain of themselves. They seem so certain of God's leadership.

Are we such a trusting people that we, too, might allow God to really be a part of the major decisions of our lives? My initial response is "No!" We will allow God to guide certain parts of our lives, but not the really important choices. We must deal with hard realities ourselves. And these realities have nothing to do with God? God is only concerned with the ethereal and spiritual, not the nuts and bolts of life. Right?

It is hard to figure out where it is that we fit in this world. We each have our own sense of purpose and being, but defining the particulars of work, relationships and commitments can be overwhelming. Trusting God to be present with us as we journey may not offer the objective certainty that we seek, but it will offer us what we can always count on—Emmanuel, God with us.

Being chosen

Mark 10:28-31

For you, was the selection of teams at recess a painful childhood experience? You may have been one of the ones chosen at the end, feeling sub-human because you could not run, hit, or catch as well as the others. Or you may have been chosen early in the process, but still aware of another child's pain at being selected with such reluctancy.

I remember early in life reading the text that said, "The first will be last and the last will be first." It was a strange idea to try and get my mind around, but every time, even until this day, I am reminded of the many who were chosen with hesitation or never chosen at all during those days of adolescence.

Playing the game of life and following all the rules does not ensure happiness. Often the results are the exact opposite. The commands that Jesus prescribes more often lead to struggle, heartache, and disappointment for those who follow the gospel faithfully. Making courageous choices based on faith may cause the world to refuse us any real playing time. We may be excluded, ridiculed and ignored because we will not stop speaking for justice and acting for the right. Family, friends and careers are not out of bounds when it comes to the walk of faith. Conflict can arise within families, circles of friends, and job-related relationships over faith issues. Such confrontations are many times the most difficult because of the depth of investment in the relationship.

Being last may not always be fun, but when it is a choice of faith, it will always be good. May we each live justly, no matter the cost in the world.

Good friends

John 15:12-l7

One of the gifts that I've come increasingly to treasure in my life is the gift of friendship. Like you, I have many different sorts of friends, old grade school buddies, former college roommates, those who share an interest. And one of the gifts of friendship that I treasure most is the gift of conversation.

A friend and I make plans to meet at a nearby cafeteria for breakfast. We may have seen each other recently; it may have been six months since we last talked. It doesn't matter. For from the moment we see each other, we begin to talk. We talk of everything, of families and jobs and the weather. We speak of our disappointments and our hopes. We allow each other a peek at our dreams, a window into our fears. We begin with breakfast, and we sit and talk until it is nearly time for lunch.

"I have called you friends," Jesus said to his disciples as well as to us. So why is it that so many of us are so formal and distant? I suspect that sometimes our prayers sound more like memos dictated to an easily offended boss than a rich, open conversation with a friend.

For me, some of the best times of prayer have come as I've stood at the kitchen sink, hands still soapy from the dishes, looking out into my backyard. It's when I've forgotten about trying to sound nice or trying to impress God (it's hard to be impressive with dishpan hands!), when I simply opened up my heart, one friend to another.

"I have called you friends," Jesus said. It is invitation as well as statement. Today, as you go about your day, take some time to talk with this friend.

Parents

1 Peter 2:9-10

In the book of Hosea, the prophet is instructed to name his daughter, Lo-ruhamah, meaning "Not pitied." Because of Israel's faithlessness, God would no longer offer them mercy. A son was to be named Lo-ammi, meaning "Not my people." God had chosen this people, but they had turned their backs on God. God would no longer claim them.

In this passage from 1 Peter, we hear the echoes of the Hosea text. But now the minor chords have been transformed. Those who were no people now are God's people. Those who once knew no mercy have now received mercy from the hands of God.

A Phil Collins song recalled hearing the words of his father, "You're no son of mine." So many of us, both as adults and children, keep working so hard to keep those words from ever happening to us, or trying to reverse them if they have. Some people choose a profession not so much out of desire or calling, but because it will make daddy (or mama) happy. Some people choose a spouse because it is the person their parents approve. Like the hamster on the wheel, they keep endlessly running but never get anywhere.

A lot of us, no matter our what relationship with our earthly parents, act the same way with God. We act out of fear. We work endlessly to prove ourselves. We do acts of faith not out of joy and calling and love, but because we hope we can convince God not to abandon us.

But you see, as 1 Peter reminds us, we don't have to prove ourselves. We don't have to earn God's mercy and love. We have been chosen. We have been redeemed. We are the children of God.

Gratitude

Psalm 135:1-4

In one respect, there are two ways of showing appreciation for a person. One is to simply say thank you, the card or note or telephone call that says "Thank you for what you've done for me, meant to me." And that is always appreciated. But I've found, both as a sender and a receiver, that the expression of thanks becomes even more meaningful as it becomes more specific. "Thank you for providing the meal—it was a big load off my mind." "Thank you for helping me sort out my options." "Thank you for your advice"—or for not giving advice at all! Recalling the reasons for our gratitude, naming them once again helps us experience all over again the caring that lay underneath the actions.

Many of our psalms, like this one, are psalms of praise. Did you notice the specificity in today's reading? The psalmist didn't just say, "Praise the Lord," but rather, "Praise the Lord, because this is what God has done." God created all the universe, and sustains all of creation. God has chosen to act in human history, calling out a people, freeing them from slavery. God's compassion does not run dry nor run out.

We also need to join with this psalmist in expressing our praise to God. We need the act of praise itself, for it turns our attention outward, it reminds us that we are not all there is in this universe. But we also need to be specific in our praise, and in doing so remind ourselves of all that God has done in this world and in our lives.

Today, take time to offer your praise to God.

Calvin's prayer

Philippians 4:8-20

One of my favorite comic strips is "Calvin and Hobbes." Calvin is, well, a rather unusual little boy and Hobbes is his stuffed but all-too real tiger. In one strip the two are talking as they walk along.

"Know what I pray for?" Calvin asks Hobbes.

"What?" the tiger replies.

"The strength to change what I can, the inability to accept what I can't, and the incapacity to know the difference."

"You should lead an interesting life," Hobbes says.

"Oh, I already do!" Calvin answers with assurance.

Paul wrote to the Philippians that he had learned to be content with whatever he had, whether it was scarcity or plenty, being hungry or being well-fed. Unlike Calvin, he could accept those things he could not change. When the church at Philippi sent him a gift, he expressed his appreciation, but also seemed to be telling them that his contentment wasn't based on their gift. He could face all circumstances equally well.

That's one of the great challenges of life, isn't it? How much time do we fret away thinking about how good our lives would be if we just had this car or that house? How much contentment do we barter away in our worry over things that are beyond our control? How many of our days do we spend saying, "If only . . . " The funny thing is, all of our worry and fretting doesn't change anything, does it? Except maybe to deprive us of a good night's sleep.

I've learned the secret, Paul said, and it had nothing to do with a stoic setting of the jaw and grim endurance of what might come. No, Paul's source of ultimate contentment came from beyond himself. His strength came from Christ, not from what he had or didn't have. And Christ would never fail him. In Christ he found the courage to change what he could and to accept what he could not change.

Clothed in joy

Matthew 22:1-14

Is there any more uncomfortable feeling than arriving at a party in the wrong attire? All the men are wearing sport coats and ties, while you're in jeans and a sport shirt. Or you're wearing your sequined dress, and everyone else is in casual clothes. Jesus spoke in this parable about some people who weren't properly dressed for the occasion

When we first begin to read this parable, it's hard to avoid a certain sense of smugness. After all, it's obviously directed to the Jews, the ones who had been promised a Messiah and then didn't recognize him when he came. They were invited to the banquet but figured they'd get around to it later. And so the servants are sent out to round up other guests. So far, so good for us.

But then comes this puzzling twist to the story. The king goes in to mingle with his new guests, and finds one man there not dressed in wedding clothes. When the king receives no reply as to why he is not properly dressed, he commands his servants to tie the man up and throw him out into the darkness.

A little harsh for violating the dress code, isn't it? But of course, that's not what the story is really all about. Eduard Schweizer in The Good News According to Matthew writes, "The guests simply do not remain as they are. The 'wedding clothes' mean something like a new mode of existence." When we receive the invitation of Christ, we are to put on our party clothes!

Jesus offers to us an invitation. Not an invitation to dry legalism but an invitation to a celebration. Attending this banquet, we should be clothed in nothing less than joy.

Don't forget to say it

1 Thessalonians 1:1-10

Dear Allen and Vivian,

Every evening when I pray, I thank God for you. When I came to this church, I immediately began to hear of your faith in Christ Jesus and how you lived out that faith in daily life. Someone told me of Allen's meeting with church members and friends at the retirement home and catching them up on the church news and letting them share reminiscences. Someone else commented on all the hard work you both put into the Sunday School classes you teach. And I had been around the church only a couple of weeks when I began to see Vivian watering and caring for the plants in church, making sure they are kept growing and beautiful. And every time I talk with either of you, you share with me stories of past and present members and how much they have given of themselves. Thank you for all the love you have shared with all of us.

Marilyn

This is a note I should have written and have not. As Paul expresses in Romans 7:19, the good I would do I don't get around to doing. How about you? Do you have pastors, friends, co-workers, those who have been important influences in your life that you should call or write—telling them of your love and prayers and thanking them for all that they have been and all that they have done? How the church at Thessalonia must have rejoiced to know that Paul had heard of the good work they were doing and that he always remembered them in his prayers. Shouldn't we bring the same kind of joy to the people in our churches today?

Happy are those

Psalm 128

This is a beatitude. Unlike Jesus' more famous ones, which make us tend to wonder what he means—how can those who mourn, because they have lost a loved one, be happy?—this one is full of promise. If we fear the Lord, we will be happy. No equivocation, no ambiguity. We will be happy.

And what does being happy mean to this Old Testament psalmist? Having a spouse and children, and looking forward to seeing your grandchildren. Very simple, really. A vision of the table of the family of God.

If this is your ideal, pray this psalm. If you are lucky enough to have a spouse and children, are in a good marriage, pray this psalm. But how many of us pray this psalm?

If this psalm describes your situation, pray it once thankfully for yourself. Then pray for all those who are in broken homes; all those who are on the street, running from abusive parents; all those whose spouses are terminally ill; all those whose children are contracting AIDS; all those who cower from abuse; all those whose lives are full of the traps and snares of tired and sick relationships.

Then go and do something for someone you know is not happy.

The depths

Psalm 130

🍂 "Out of the depths I cry to you, O Lord."

For some it steals in quietly, like the fading of the light at nightfall. Slowly a great depression creeps in, and the days seem gray and empty and ever so difficult to get through. The night seems complete, and some days you wonder if the day will ever break again.

For others, it comes with the swiftness of a blow. The bad news comes, news about the medical tests or the accident or the job. And suddenly it's as if you are in a new country, one in which the roads are difficult to travel, and the directions sometimes unclear. Questions of "Why?" and "What now?" buzz about like a housefly that won't leave.

For still others, the depths are more like an emptiness. The problem is not that the feelings are painful; they just aren't there. The faith that once brought life and joy now seems to be but a hollow shell.

Sooner or later life brings all of us to the depths, the deep places of grief or depression or crisis. In such times, we do well to return to this psalm, to mingle our prayers with those of the psalmist. "Lord, hear my voice!"

From the depths, the psalmist prays, pleads, waits and hopes. From the depths, we lift our voices as well, for our hope is the same, our Lord is the same. The Lord will hear our cries. And the Lord will remember us, even in the depths.

"I wait for the Lord, my soul waits, and in his word I hope."

Hearing and speaking

Mark 7:31-37

Working with stroke patients, I became fascinated with questions of hearing and speaking. If they were comatose, could they hear me? If they could not speak, could they still communicate? They challenged all of my preconceived notions of communication.

In today's text, we once again have the images of hearing and speaking. Jesus heals a deaf man not only by opening his ears, but also by healing his speech that has been mute. The man not only hears, but speaks plainly.

In today's text, we have images of the opening of deaf ears and mute tongues. And I look at my life and wonder what is blocking my hearing. What gets in the way of hearing God's call in my life? What gets in the way of truly hearing another person, what they are saying about themselves and what they are trying to tell me about myself? Sometimes it is my fear of what I will hear if my ears are unstopped. Sometimes it is my preconceived notions of what I ought to hear.

And some things prevent me from speaking plainly. I'm not talking about the plain speech that was the goal when I went to speech therapy as a child. No, I mean speaking plainly the truth of our lives, the truth of what we see and hear and feel. I may be afraid of what others will think of me. I may not believe that my words are important. Perhaps I tried to speak in the past, but no one listened.

Today, look at your own life. Where are the deaf places that need to be unstopped? Where are the mute places that need to be set free? Take some time to talk with and listen to God in prayer.

What lies behind

Philippians 3:12-16

❧ "Forgetting what lies behind" (v. 13) does not mean exactly what it says. Clearly, Paul has not literally forgotten his past. In fact, in Philippians 3:4-6 he describes his former situation. His roots were completely Jewish. His religious affiliation had been with the most rigorous of Pharisees. He'd lived a legalistic life, and been instrumental in persecuting the church. Not just in this letter, but also on other occasions, Paul remembered that persecution of the Body of Christ of which he had been chief agent (for example, Acts 22:3ff, Acts 26:4ff, 1 Cor 15:9). Forget? No, he remembered—probably with tears.

However, he did not allow his past to shackle his future. That future was filled with Christ. His past was "forgotten" in the sense that it did not taint the spiritual reality of his present commitment to the gospel.

How often do we allow the sin of our past to impede us? We feel guilty. We feel shame. We feel embarrassment. We feel unworthy. We feel useless.

That is not Paul's way, nor the way of the gospel. Our sins are forgiven by the grace of God in Christ Jesus. We are freed from guilt and our sins. In God's eyes we are beloved and worthy.

Let us say, "Yes, I have sinned, but God is greater than my sin. He calls me on, so on I will go until in the end I will receive the prize—everlasting communion with God."

Freedom for

1 Corinthians 9:16-23

Freedom is a word that has been closely related to the United States of America. Out of a desire for freedom from monarchical rule, this country was born. But freedom has also been one of our most difficult struggles—not only in the wars we have fought, but also in the thousands of conflicts of everyday life. What does it mean to be free? What happens when my freedom impinges on your freedom? What are the limits to freedom of speech and freedom of expression? Any new law in the US is guaranteed to meet with stiff resistance if it appears to limit individual freedoms. We have recognized that in order to live together as a society, there must be some limits. We keep trying to work out a good way of defining and establishing those limits.

Paul knew something about freedom. In his conversion, he was set free from the Law that he had followed so vigorously. And yet the paradox is that he was set free to serve. His was not only a freedom *from*, it was a freedom *for*. Paul's overriding concern wasn't defending his personal freedom, it was proclaiming the gospel. And if that meant keeping some parts of the Law in order to be able to reach those still under the Law, then he would do it. If it meant giving up his Jewish identity to step into the world of the Gentiles, he would do it. Paul wasn't simply going with the prevailing winds, he was freely choosing to do what was necessary to reach those for whom Christ died, Jew and Gentile alike. In his conversion, Paul was set free, but then chose to become a servant of Christ.

What are you free for?

Dreams

Luke 9:1-6

I enjoy talking with people about our dreams for our lives. But for some of us it's much easier to list all the reasons why a particular dream will never come true than the reasons why it can become reality. Perhaps it's easier to see road blocks than to see all of the doors that are open, even if they are opened only a little bit.

When Jesus commissioned the disciples, he gave to them authority over the demons and power to heal diseases. He sent them to proclaim the good news in their words and in their healing work. Yet at the same time, he didn't give them so many things that seem to us to be necessary, things that were basic . . . no extra clothes, no extra food, no American Express card. They were empowered with a tremendous gift, but they were also dependent upon others. Strange contradiction, isn't it?

More and more, I am coming to believe that God truly does provide everything we need to do what we are called to do. But first we have to separate what we are called by God to do from what others simply think we ought to do. (Or what we think we ought to do in order to be well-liked.) The second step is to separate what we truly need from what we'd like to have. Sometimes, you see, the roadblocks are of our own making.

What about you? What has God called you to do with your life? What has God called you to do with this day? Accept God's empowering gifts, and ask for the faith to trust and the grace to hope.

It's simple

2 Kings 5:1-14

He was a lawyer for an agency in the United States government—and an unbeliever. He was also a good husband and father, and so accompanied his wife to Sunday School and church each week.

One Sunday the adult class was discussing salvation. The teacher stressed the point that, although regular church attendance, giving, and working for the church are commendable, not one of them produces salvation. The only basis for salvation, he said, is belief—belief in the Lord Jesus Christ.

The lawyer lingered after class. "Do you mean it's that simple?" he asked incredulously.

"It's that simple," was the reply.

"Well, it seems to me there ought to be more to it than that." The two arranged to meet for lunch so the teacher could explain.

Naaman, the Syrian leper, made the same mistake. The cure for his leprosy should be more involved than dipping himself in the turbid, muddy Jordan River, as the prophet Elisha prescribed. After all, if dipping in a river could effect a cure, it would be far better to immerse himself in the Abana or the Pharpar, two clear streams of his native Syria. And there ought to be some hand-waving or other ritual.

Fortunately, Naaman's servants prevailed upon him to obey the prophet of God. The proud commander dipped—and was healed. No leprosy, no blemish, no scars.

As with Naaman's leprosy, the cure for our sin is simple, obedient faith— faith plus nothing.

Incidentally, the lawyer also found his cure—in simple belief.

Forgetting the past

Isaiah 43:18-25

There are times when forgetting can be hazardous to our health: forgetting to take an important heart or blood pressure medicine; forgetting to look both ways before pulling out of a side street; forgetting to cut off the electric power before repairing the stove.

There are other times when forgetting brings unpleasant consequences: forgetting to mail our income tax by April 15; forgetting a birthday or an anniversary; forgetting an important business meeting.

But there are times when forgetting is the best thing to do. Past failures and past sins cannot be called back for alteration. Automobile manufacturers may recall a certain model to make needed changes, but we cannot undo an act, no matter how fervently we wish to. As Omar Khayyam observed,

"The Moving Finger writes and having writ, Moves on; not all your Piety nor Wit Shall lure it back to cancel half a Line, Nor all your Tears wash out a Word of it."

Though we can't change the past, we are commanded by God to forget many unalterable things—and not to dwell on them. Morbid guilt and self-condemnation can only cripple us. Once truly repented and confessed, our sins are erased by the blood of Christ. God is eager to forgive our transgressions. This was God's purpose in sending Jesus. God has promised to remember our sins no more!

Fear and trust

Psalm 27

Many psychologists tell us that the dominant emotion of our society is fear. The fear of falling, they say, appears very early in life. Then there comes fear of school, fear of failure, fear of not finding a job, fear of losing a job, fear of aging, fear of disability, fear of dependency, fear of death—and a host of others.

Our age has been called the Aspirin Age and the Age of Anxiety because of the stress and fear that dominate our lives. Increasingly sophisticated technology that displaces workers, the threat of nuclear warfare, the outbreak of diseases—all menace us. Even worse is our realization that we have little or no control over many of these threats.

In Psalm 27, David gives the timeless antidote to fear—trust in God, trust based on his experiences of God's deliverance in the past and God's promises for the future. David had been preserved through many threats and dangers. He had also received God's covenant promise to make of his line a dynasty that would last forever.

We, too, have been delivered by our God from the dominion of sin and darkness and have been brought "through many dangers, toils, and snares." And from the same God that David knew we have the promise, "I will never leave you or forsake you."

As David discovered, the only sure cure for fear is a complete trust in the God who loves us.

The "C" word

Psalm 105:1 -11

At sixteen, Jim told his mother he had found a job. "All I have to do is pick up the waste in the yard every week, and he'll pay me twenty-five dollars!" His mother was puzzled. "Whose yard?" she asked. "The lumber yard," he answered. Surprised, his mother said, "Do you know what that means? Are you ready to make this kind of commitment?"

Cathy was having second thoughts about the wedding tomorrow. A lifelong, responsible relationship? She was only twenty-five; she had lived so little! What was she giving up? How could she handle the responsibility? Had she rushed this entire thing?

"This position requires a greater commitment to the company, Jan. There will be travel, and some overtime as well. Still, the rewards will be worth it: more money, of course, but also learning opportunities, faster promotions and better benefits. What do you think? Can you commit?"

We all struggle when making commitments or entering into covenants. In today's scripture, a spiritual covenant is handed down to us with encouragement to do something about it. We find statements that lead us to reflect upon our own commitment experiences, our own traditions, and how those traditions affect our spirituality. What connections do we have with that long-ago covenant? What can we do, and how?

O patient and persistent God,
    too often we do not remember
    your wonderful work,
    nor do we sing praises to you,
    or glory in your holy name.
As we seek you through the days,
    let our hearts rejoice in that seeking.
As we seek to make our commitment deepen and grow,
    guide our studies;
    be present in all our decisions.
    May our faith become real.

Fish in the sea

Luke 5:1-11

Peter had been up all night. He was exhausted and doubt-filled. He was ready to take a break, get a bath, eat breakfast, nap. Then Jesus climbed on board and the process of a miracle began.

Jesus asked the weary Peter to move the boat back into the water, away from the shore. He used the vessel as a pulpit, then he wanted to go fishing. Had I been in Peter's sandals that day, I think I would have lost my cool. The hour was late, the method wasn't working, the effort had been made, and home was looking real good. But stressed as he was, Peter obliged and obeyed the one he called "Master." Useless as it seemed, Peter was willing to make an effort; he was willing to attempt what seemed to be hopeless.

Again, the nets went overboard and into the barren lake. KABOOM! Suddenly, there were so any fish that the nets broke and two boats began to sink. Peter fell to his knees, realizing that a miracle had occurred.

The true miracle, however, was not the amazing catch that day. The true miracle was in Peter's obedience to Jesus. He had been willing to make another effort after struggling all night. When Jesus asked it of him, tired as he was, Peter was prepared to try again. For most of us, the disaster of life is that we give up just one effort too soon. Peter had been willing to attempt what seemed hopeless. We may hesitate or completely stop because the time or circumstances are not opportune. When we wait for a perfect situation, we never begin at all.

Cousins

Luke 8:19-21

My brother was home during a college break. One day a neighbor asked him to pick up her daughter when classes dismissed at the local elementary school. Jeffrey was glad to do the favor.

Our family, the preacher's family, had been counted as a part of the child's family and community since before her birth. We had been included in their extended family gatherings, had worshiped together, played together, and buried loved ones together.

When my brother entered the classroom that day, the teacher asked who he was. Without hesitation Susan replied, "Oh, he's my cousin," and so far as she knew, he was.

William Barclay writes, "The deepest relationship of life is not merely a blood relationship; it is the relationship of mind to mind, heart to heart. It is when people have common aims, common principles, common interests, a common goal that they become really and truly kin."

Susan and her family found that kinship with our family, and vice versa. Jesus found kinship, not with his biological family, for they had considered him mad (Mark 3:21), but with his disciples. He claimed kinship with "those who hear the word of God and do it." As a part of God's family, we must realize that Jesus demands a loyalty that surpasses all earthly loyalties. He gave his life for each of us and he requires nothing less in return.

Also, we must realize that when a person gives one's self completely to Christ, he or she becomes a member of a family whose boundaries are the earth. Any losses are counterbalanced by the gains. Those who seek the will of God through Jesus Christ enter into a family that includes not just blood kin, but all the saints in earth and heaven. What a lineage!

Challenge

Matthew 19:27-30

"Ask not what your country can do for you—ask what you can do for your country." John F. Kennedy re-directed his listeners that day. He challenged folks to ask not what they could get but what they could give. It was a great speech. It was needed by the people of that day.

It is a great speech still. It is needed by the people of this day. In the '90s, we shop for cars, jobs, churches, relationships and anything else with one question in mind, "What's in it for me?" Sadly, this is a self-centered, self-serving way to live.

But then, humanity has been selfish throughout history. In this scripture, we find Peter, a close disciple of Christ, raising the same ugly question, "What do we get out of following you?"

Jesus responded to Peter, not with scolding and rebuking, but with surprising patience. He honored Peter through the gift of a direct, specific answer. Perhaps Jesus suspected this troubling issue to be in the hearts of those listening. Perhaps he senses it in our hearts today.

Jesus re-directed his listeners from a self-centered stance to one of finding value in a personal and sacrificial relationship with him. He encouraged his followers to "faith it," to hold on for a greater reward some time in the future. Jesus urged us to value the virtue of a humble attitude, reminding us that the last will be first.

Today, as we wonder "What's in it for me?", may we find the courage to "faith it" in the meantime, and may God give the grace to save us from ourselves. Let us learn to ask not what our Lord can do for us, but what we can do for our Lord.

Missed opportunities

1 Corinthians 7:29-31

"Delay is the best way to kill a great idea or movement."

The speaker caught my attention; I carry around a few of my own memories of missed opportunities. I could have resolved a conflict or made a friend if only I had seized the moment. I could have succeeded in a particular project if only I hadn't wasted so much time waiting around for the conditions to fall perfectly into place.

If I have turned my will and my life over to the care of God, I now know that part of my responsibility in the process of journeying with God is to stay on the move. It is crucial that I stay awake and aware of how short the journey really is and how little time I really do have to accomplish my assignment.

It is important for me to stay focused on my task, learning to discern the difference between the urgent things that sap my strength and dilute my efforts and the important things God is calling me to accomplish. I don't need to get tunnel vision, but I do need to make sure that I channel my energies in the most effective and efficient ways, that I be with the people God has called me to be with, that I stay attentive to the pathway that God has assigned to me.

I want to look back over my life and my days and be able to say that I seized the moment and that I did not miss my pathway because I delayed. In the few minutes that I have been given to live, I want to do what I was created to do. Someday, I'd like to hear that blessing, "Well done, good and faithful servant."

In the meantime, I have my assignment.

God's timing

Mark 1:14-20

"God is never late," Jeanette Clift George says, "but He has missed a great many opportunities to be early!"

I laughed, but then I wanted to cry, for I have spent my lifetime wrestling with God about God's timetable. When a new challenge emerges, I forget what I have learned and think that I can take over the timing of circumstances.

It is important on the journey for me to remember what part of the responsibility is mine and what part is God's. I get in trouble when I try to take over God's jobs; I usually do that when I think my job is too hard or too insignificant.

God is, after all, the Lord of time, and sees the whole picture of creation, not just my small part of it. God sees all of time, from beginning to end, and is concerned for all of us. Most of the time, I wish I had my personal God, assigned to the task of making my life work out exactly as I want and when I want it to! I forget that God is at work to bring about God's purposes, not mine, on God's timetable.

And so, periodically, I go in for tutorials. Forgetting that I am not God, I have to take some remedial lessons. My task is to seek the kingdom; that is, it is mine to give up trying to control life and let God be in charge. After all, the call is for me to follow God, not the other way around! And then, after that, it is my responsibility to declare the Good News, to be a fisher of persons in whatever way I have been equipped.

And on the way, I can be comforted that God is exactly on time.

A thankful heart

Psalm 111

"I will give thanks to the Lord with my whole heart." A thankful heart is a quality we all need to cultivate. In doing so, we acknowledge the greatness and goodness of God and accept our own finitude.

Benjamin Franklin recalled an experience from his boyhood. He told about the old salt barrel that stood in the corner of the kitchen. Meat was taken from the barrel daily to provide for the family's needs. Franklin's father prayed at every meal, "Thank thee, Father, for the meat thou hast laid before us." One day young Franklin managed enough courage to suggest, "Father, why don't we say thanks over the whole barrel one time and be done with it?" Commenting on the experience years later, Franklin said he would never forget the stern rebuke of his father for such presumptuous ingratitude.

Franklin's experience was not unlike my own. Times were hard on the farm during my childhood. We always had too much month at the end of the money! One Christmas I asked for a basketball. When I opened my present I found an inexpensive dime store ball. This was all my parents could afford. Disappointed, I lashed out at my mother, "I told you I wanted a basketball!"

Later, as I walked past my mother's bedroom, I heard her crying as she prayed, "Lord, we are doing our best to provide for our children. Help them be grateful for what they have." I learned an important lesson that day. God wants us to be grateful for everything, great and small.

Paul reminded us, "In everything give thanks, for this is the will of God in Christ Jesus concerning you" (1 Thess 5:18, KJV). Make a list of all the persons and blessings you are thankful for today.

Folly

1 Corinthians 1:18-31

Archaeologists have discovered a drawing and inscription in what was evidently a room beneath the imperial palace in ancient Rome. Apparently the drawing was intended to be a caricature of the crucifixion of Jesus. It depicts a man's body hanging on a cross, but the head is that of a donkey.

To the left of the cross is the figure of a young man with his hand raised as if he is worshiping the figure on the cross. The inscription below the drawing reads, "Alexamenos worships his god."

The room where the drawing was found was very likely used as a prison. With a little imagination we can construct the situation. A young man named Alexamenos was a Christian. Perhaps he was a servant in the imperial palace or even a prisoner. This much is clear: Alexamenos was being mocked and ridiculed by those not in sympathy with his worship of Jesus Christ.

This drawing is a vivid illustration of Paul's comment concerning the cross, "For the word of the cross is folly to those who are perishing, but to us who are being saved it is the power of God" (1 Cor 1:18, RSV). Paul added that the cross was a stumbling block to the Jew who expected a military messiah. To the enlightened Greek it was sheer foolishness. Despite these obstacles, Paul concluded that wherever the word of the cross is proclaimed, God's life-changing power is released.

The cross may still be regarded as a stumbling block to some. For those who have the eyes of faith, however, the cross means that life can be different. God is able to replace fear, guilt and despair with courage, peace and hope. Yes, there is power in the cross!

Neighbors

Luke 6:39-42

A traveler was seeking a place where his family might settle. He stopped in a rural community and engaged a farmer in conversation. "What kind of people live around here?" he inquired. The farmer answered with a question, "Well, friend, what kind of people live in the community you came from?" Frowning, the inquirer replied, "Oh, they were terrible people. Liars, cheats, gossips." The farmer sadly shook his head. "You might as well move on," he urged, "because that's the way people are around here, too!"

Later, a second traveler looking for a new home stopped by. He asked the same farmer about residents there. "Well, tell me about the people where you came from," the farmer prodded. "Oh, they were simply wonderful," the traveler responded. "They were the most thoughtful, generous, loving folk you could imagine. We certainly hated to leave them." "That's great," beamed the farmer, "because that's the way people are around here, too! You might as well unpack and settle down."

Could it be that the faults we condemn in others are the same shortcomings we tend to overlook in ourselves? Our judgments about others may be like looking though binoculars. We look through the small lenses at their failures in order to magnify them and bring them into sharper focus. But we view our own faults through the large lenses, thus making them seem smaller and less significant.

Jesus warned against a critical, judgmental attitude. To make his point, he used a ludicrous illustration about a person with a plank in his or her eye trying to remove a speck or splinter from a neighbor's eye. Clarence Jordan observed that the splinter probably came from the accuser's plank! Radical self-surgery is required before we are qualified to help others with their failures.

Sleeping on a stormy night

Luke 6:43-49

A certain farmer interviewed prospective employees. The worker who most impressed him was a strong-looking man with a relaxed manner and a winning smile. However, his responses to the farmer's inquiry were quite unusual.

"I need somebody to look after livestock."

The prospective hand answered, "I can sleep well on a stormy night."

"Carpentry work is required and there are fences to be mended."

Again came the reply, "I can sleep well on a stormy night."

"I expect a straight furrow. How are you with a plow?"

"I can sleep well on a stormy night," repeated the hand. Although perplexed, the farmer hired him and he did an outstanding job.

One night a storm came. Lightning flashed and thunder rolled. Wind shook the house and rain descended in torrents. The farmer jumped out of bed to summon the hired man. Alas, he was sleeping soundly and could not be awakened. So the farmer checked on things alone. The horses were in their stalls in the barn. The windows in the henhouse were shut. Tools were in their proper places. Everything was in perfect readiness for the storm.

The next morning the farmer remarked to the hired man, "We had quite a storm last night." "I didn't notice," the hand replied. "Storms don't bother me." Then the farmer understood the meaning of the statement, "I can sleep well on a stormy night."

The hired hand had a marvelous philosophy of life. Storms will come. The time to prepare for them is in advance.

Faith-giving

Mark 12:41-44

The concept of the tithe has been ingrained into me. When my parents received their box of offering envelopes, I got one too. As soon as I earned my first dollar, I began putting my own money in the offering. My folks did not spend time with the "before or after taxes debate." They just gave according to the need. The family budget suggested in an article that I read would have galled them. For a family of five with a monthly income of over $4,000.00, the article recommended a donation of $25.00. That wouldn't get God's commendation where I was brought up. "As a minimum, compute the tithe if you expect God's blessings!" screams my vestiges of legalism. "Forget the amount," pleads our text. Forget about giving in expectancy of reaping a larger benefit—that's investment business. Consider giving out of faith— that's gratitude.

I have some acquaintances who decided a long time ago the minimal amount of income required for them to live with a degree of comfort without living in luxury, and to give the rest away. When they began the practice, their income was less than $20,000.00 per year. Their income is now six figures, but with some adjustment for inflation, they continue to live on their previously "fixed income," giving away the remainder. The husband once told me that the widow in this parable embarrassed them. They decided what they could live on, and gave away the rest. The widow gave away everything she had, and decided to live on the rest. That's the issue of pride again. The lessons on tithing from my childhood have become prisoners of my pride now that I'm an adult.

O Lord, teach me to be unselfish when it comes to serving you.

Build a perfect friend

Psalm 145

What do you look for in a relationship? Whether it be a romantic relationship or a good friend, what qualities are important to you? One of the group exercises that I've done with groups is called "Build A Perfect Friend Pyramid." I give them a collection of "building blocks," rectangular-shaped pieces of paper labeled with different qualities such as honesty, sense of humor, athletic ability, shared interests, smart, even good hair! I then ask them to choose thirteen out of the twenty or so items that are most important to them in choosing a friend. Then they arrange the blocks in a pyramid, with the most important quality on top. Much to my relief, no one yet has chosen "good hair" as a sought-after quality in a friend!

So what do you look for in a relationship? One of the things that strikes me about this psalm is how many different words it uses to describe what God is like. A partial listing includes: great, gracious, compassionate, merciful, loving, slow to anger, faithful, just and kind.

Read the list again, slowly. Or re-read the psalm and make your own list. Read it for what is there and for what is not there. Words like demeaning, oppressive, belittling, capricious, and punitive are conspicuously absent.

Read the list again, slowly. This is the God who is here for us and with us. This is the God who waits to listen to us as we pray, to speak to us as we listen. This is the God we can trust with our lives.

Widows, orphans, and aliens

Jeremiah 22:1-5

Aliens. Orphans. Widows. Over and over again we find these three groups of people mentioned in the words of the prophets. Specifically, the quality of the devotion of God's people will be measured by the care that they give to these people.

They were all people who had no rights and no standing in the community. Orphans had no parents and widows had no husbands to provide for them, to protect them. Foreigners had no place of their own in the community. They were the strangers, the aliens. In short, the widows, orphans and aliens were the easiest people to take advantage of, to harm, to treat unjustly. For how can people complain if they have no voice? How can they make a change if they have no power?

Over and over again the prophets remind us that the people of God are called to speak for those who have no voice, to care for those who have no protectors, to stand up for those who have no power. Our worship is play-acting at best, and at worst a sham, if we do not reach out to these, our brothers and sisters.

They're still among us, you know, these orphans, aliens and widows. They are here as immigrants, Cambodians and Mexicans and a dozen other nationalities. They are here as migrant workers. They are here as children who do not have votes. They are here as single parents struggling to raise their families. They are here as elderly people faced with too many changes and too few resources. These people we are to receive into our lives with justice and mercy.

What would Jeremiah say today if he were to walk the streets of your town, the corridors of your business, the aisles of your church?

Vacation by the sea

Psalm 93

I've had the usual rush of things that must be done before I can leave for even a few days of vacation. The work to be taken care of. The newspapers to be stopped. The laundry to be done. But now I am here, and something within me slows down, eases up, and relaxes.

I stand out on the balcony and watch the ocean waves caress the beach. I listen to the rhythm of the breakers. I squint my eyes and look along the horizon. I take deep, glad breaths of salt air. And something within me shifts.

I stand before the "mighty waters," and am silenced by the wonder of it all. There is much mystery still in this world. There is much that is still beyond our power and our control. And there is still God.

For the power and the majesty and the mystery and the beauty of the oceans are but a small reminder of the power, majesty, mystery, and beauty of God.

Today, take a moment to be still, to let wonder invite you to worship.

Held in the arms

Psalm 131

Seeing the black and white images on the movie screen, I suddenly remembered the feeling. I was two years old, and it was Sunday morning. I know it was Sunday, because I was dressed in my patent leather shoes and my hat and enough ruffles under my dress to make me six inches taller when I sat down.

I was in the front yard of our old house, wandering about in the unsteady and random ways of two-year-olds. Suddenly I stopped, and my whole purpose and direction changed in a moment. My dad had walked out the front door. I ran to him as fast as my chubby little legs would take me, and he swooped me up in his arms to what seemed an impossibly tall height.

Years later I was watching the movie and I remembered. I remembered how absolutely safe I felt. I might have been off the ground, in the air, but it was okay. Because I knew whose arms held me. Years later I felt again the warmth and the peace of utter trust. It was okay, because I knew whose arms held me.

Trust. It's what this psalm is all about. Like the child asleep in her mother's arms, the psalmist is relaxed and at peace. For he knows in whose arms he is held. And those arms will not fail him.

So it is for us. For we, too, are cradled in the loving arms of God. And so when the pace becomes a bit too frantic today, or your enemies a bit too vocal, or your problems a bit too menacing, remember. Remember whose you are. And remember in whose arms you are held, in whose love you are kept.

It's time

Romans 13-14

The woman looks at her husband. "It's time," she says. "The baby's coming. It's time to go to the hospital."

The family has been told of the death, and they have cried and grieved and signed all of the right papers. Finally one of them speaks up. "It's time," he says softly, "It's time to go home."

The husband looks at his wife over the dinner table. "It's time," he says. "It's time for me to change jobs."

It's time. How many times do we hear that? Sometimes it's an ordinary kind of time, like time for the concert to begin or time for the plane to take off. But these other occasions are different. They are not *chronos* time, tick-tock, clock kind of time, but *kairos* time. The New Testament speaks of it as "the right time," the "fullness of time." It is *kairos* time that Paul is talking about in this passage. You know what the time is, he says, and he doesn't mean that your watch is up to the minute. No, you know in your heart and in your soul. It's time. It's time to put away an old life. It's time to start living as God's children.

"It's time," she said as they were discussing an old and worn-out self image. "It's time to let it go. It's time to let God heal that part of you."

What about you? Perhaps it's time for you to let go of something . . . an old hurt, an old prejudice, an old way of viewing the world or yourself that gets in the way of God's work in and through you. Or perhaps it's time for an embrace to embrace the joy and the peace that God offers.

In the stillness today, listen. It's time.

List your strengths

Psalm 8

I've done the exercise with several different kinds of groups, teenagers, adults, folks inside the church and out. But the process is always strikingly similar. I ask each person to list their strengths and their "growing edges" (what others close to us may call our faults). It's easy enough to list what we need to work on. That side of the page is quickly finished. But listing strengths involves much hemming and hawing and chewing on pencils.

Perhaps it's because some of us were taught not to brag on ourselves, and affirmation and celebration have become hopelessly confused with bragging. Or perhaps it's because we hear the other side much more frequently. The boss who reminds us that we procrastinate. The spouse who reminds us that we forgot to pick up the dry cleaning again this week. The kids who throw the brilliance and perfection of their friend's parents in our faces. The people who laugh when we wonder out loud about joining the choir. The popular magazines that remind us we are a bit too fat or a bit too wrinkled, or that we are wearing last year's hairstyle. It's easy to get the message.

In fact, it's so easy to get that message that sometimes it stands in the way of hearing the truth. We all have those areas of our lives that we need to work on. (If you don't, then kindly keep it to yourself!) But sometimes we get so focused on all we *aren't* that we forget what we *are*.

We have been created in the image of God. And God said, "That's good." Beneath it all, beyond it all, you are a beautiful, beloved creation of God. And that is what matters most.

Learning from the other

Luke 7:1-10

And who will teach us what it means to be faithful?

I was spending a couple of days at a Catholic retreat center. The director of the center (a nun) greeted me with a smile at breakfast the morning of my second day. It seems that she had been watching a game show the night before, and the question put to the contestant was to name a non-Christian religion. "Catholic," the woman answered. "What denomination are you?" the game show host asked. "Southern Baptist," the woman replied. "Well, I think that Catholics are Christians, too," the host said gently.

Fortunately, my friend laughed as she told me. I'll have to admit that I was groaning inside with embarrassment.

Usually it's not that blatant. But far too often we learn somewhere along the way to regard other members of the body of Christ—our brothers and our sisters—with suspicion. If they are of the faith, then they surely are not as much of the faith as we are. Surely they have nothing to teach us about what it means to be Christian, what it means to be faithful. So we deprive ourselves of much that could inform and enrich our faith.

And who will teach us what it means to be faithful?

This text demands that we take the question a bit further. This Roman officer had no religious pedigree, no standing within the community of God's people. He was an outsider. Yet it was of him that Jesus said, "Never have I seen such faith!"

Could it be that someone beyond our neat circle is an example for us? Could it be that an outsider could teach us? Could it be?

And who will teach us what it means to be faithful?

Talking to yourself

Psalm 146

Spoken words exert great power on our lives. Maybe that's why I talk to myself. What I say out loud affects my outlook on a situation. I heard about a man who was asked, "Sir, why is it that you are always talking to yourself?" "Well, you see, it's like this," came the reply. "I like to talk to an intelligent person and I like to hear an intelligent person talk." Sounds like foolishness, but there can be a trace of truth in such a response if we are reflecting on the majesty and mercy of God. Historically, Psalm 146 was spoken aloud as part of morning prayers. It served to establish the framework within which an individual could understand the events which would follow during the day. Not such a bad idea!

Ever had folk disappoint you by not keeping their commitments to you? Then start off the day by talking about how God always keeps faith with you, although you may have to deal with a disappointment or two in human relationships.

Ever get down about the lack of justice in the world and in the community where you live? Then talk about serving a God who desires justice and cares for the oppressed.

Ever think that maybe you should not be bothered with the concerns of the strangers who cross your path—think that maybe you can turn a profit by taking advantage of their situation in some way? Well, talk about how such wicked plotting will be brought to ruin by the Lord.

So talk to yourself this morning. "Now, self, you just believe in the Lord, for the Lord is going to keep faith with you today and with those whom you encounter!"

Walking in light

John 8:12-20

Last year, our Deep South city was hit by a blizzard. Power lines snapped and came tumbling down. The whole city lay in darkness. For six long days and nights, we had no lights. We scurried around for candles, oil lamps and flashlights with working batteries, grateful even for the flickering light of the fireplace.

Life was unalterably changed. Our whole pattern of doing things was disrupted because of this lack of electricity. We worked hard during the daylight hours, chopping wood, arranging our light sources, getting ready for the coming of the dark.

The day the lights came on, a cheer went up from house to house in our neighborhood. We had light, and life could become normal once more.

Jesus said that he was the light of the world. He did not say that he was the light of the church or of America. He stated it clearly. "I am the light of the world."

I like the next phrase, "Whoever follows me will never walk in darkness but will have the light of life." Notice Jesus' words: "the light of life." I have learned the hard way that my plants shrivel and die in the wintertime if they only stand in the dark corners of the room. Without light they cannot survive. Are we not the same? Sometimes we find ourselves looking for light in strange quarters. But today we pause to remember Jesus' words, "I am the light of the world."

Let us move closer to our source of power. We will find our nights and days illumined. We will find a never-failing beacon for our winding, twisting journeys. But more than that, we will discover that everything looks different in the light he brings. Jesus is the light of life.

Names

Proverbs 22:1-2, 8-9

Ever doubt the importance of names? Let's list a few names and think of the emotions they stir as you read them.

Mother Teresa
Jim Bakker
Jezebel
Lee Harvey Oswald
Martin Luther King, Jr.
Audrey Hepburn
Robert Oppenheimer
Dr. Seuss
Dietrich Bonhoeffer
Eleanor Roosevelt
Charles Manson
Billy Graham

Some names stretch us and make us feel good. Other names frighten us and cause us to wonder about the human spirit.

In the Old and New Testaments, names were important. People were given names that would mark them for life. The challenge was to live up to the names they were given.

Once Alexander the Great caught one of his soldiers sleeping on duty. He was furious. From his horse he peered down at the soldier. "What is your name?" he asked. The soldier said, "My name is Alexander." Alexander the Great leaned over and knocked him to the ground. "Either change your name or change what you are."

Jesus calls us children of God. He also said that it does not yet appear what we shall be. So we ponder the meaning of this very great grace. The challenge is to live up to our names.

Second greatest commandment

James 2:8-13

James is one of the most ethical books in the Bible. Ethics deals with the do's and the don'ts, the actions we live by. James is a book of deeds and not simply words.

Love your neighbor as yourself, he says. This is a very tall order. Let's reverse the order of the command. If we truly love ourselves, we will love our neighbors.

Love yourself. Buried within all of us is a sense of unworthiness. Despite all the literature to the contrary, self-hate is epidemic. We are to treat ourselves as well as we would a stranger. Arthur Miller said there comes a time when we all have to take ourselves in our own arms. This love of self begins with the knowledge that God loves us. John 3:16 bears our names. Begin to operate out of this love of self. What would it mean for you to love yourself today?

Love your neighbor. Now move out into your world. Think of the people you will touch in one way or another today. The one who sits across from you at breakfast. The people at work. Someone on the telephone. Strangers on the street. One epistle says, "Be ye kind." Why? Because it's rough out there. People are having a hard time. Some spark of recognition may just mean the difference between life and death for somebody.

James ends this passage by saying, show mercy. Jesus, at the beginning of his ministry, had already said it. Blessed are they who know the mercy of God, for they shall show mercy. Give yourself this gift of mercy and let the ripples in the stream widen and widen.

Love is what you do

James 3:13-18

My grandmother told me that as her father got older, his hands got so shaky that he had trouble doing most mechanical things. Things such as shaving, which you and I may take for granted, turned into dangerous chores for him. Of all his children, it was my grandmother who would shave him. She did not go unnoticed or unappreciated, because one day he told her, "I love you best because you shave me."

Love is expressed through concrete action. Love does not always get positive responses, and sometimes our love is not returned or even acknowledged.

Does that mean that we have wasted our time? By no means. Jesus told us that we are to love even when that love is not recognized. Over the years, many in the church have confused people about some issues, making certain people feel unwelcome in the church. We have often followed the dictates of culture rather than the commandments of our Lord. We have hated in the name of love. Slavery, racism, sexism, war, and poverty have all flourished because of our unwillingness to truly love one another.

Just as my grandmother concretely showed love for her father, we must be willing to act sacrificially and unselfishly. The church must run counter to our culture. As James points out, it is not what we say but what we do that shows our true heart.

Pray that God will open avenues of service for you so that you will truly be an instrument of peace in your community. May you find the way of wisdom to be a clear path which leads you straight to your hurting neighbor.

Eldad and Medad

Numbers 11:24-30

What an intriguing story!

A group of elders had been chosen by Moses to receive the spirit of the Lord in a meeting. Once they received the spirit, they prophesied—evidently among themselves—but only once.

Meanwhile Eldad and Medad, two fellows who missed Moses' first cut and remained back at the campsite, discovered that some of God's spirit—whoa!—had landed on them, too! So, of course, they prophesied, which means they got visibly excited, even emotional about God and being God's people. Right in front of everybody! They must have made quite an impression because one of the anxious witnesses reported to Moses that some unsanctioned religious zeal was taking place back home.

Now this witness probably thought Moses would break a tablet over this, but instead Moses responded by saying, "What's the problem? I wish every last one of you would become a prophet—we might really see God's spirit then!" Three cheers for Moses.

I wonder, though, whatever happened to Eldad and Medad once Moses and the elders returned?

I think they've been around on occasion. Someone usually tattles on them. Or ignores them. Or locks them up. Or assassinates them. Or kicks them out of the church.

When we've gathered our tent and designated who our prophets will be, we get uneasy with anyone who wants to "prophesy" outside the lines. Perhaps we assume that God's got only so much spirit to go around. Or perhaps we're afraid that if God's spirit can land on anyone, it might get all over us, too.

God forbid!

Wow!

Psalm 113

Who is like the Lord our God? I have a good friend with whom I have shared a number of experiences working among people who are homeless. One of the men we came to know from our association with one shelter in Louisville, Kentucky, managed to leave behind a past life of substance abuse, complete a course of vocational training, secure a full-time job, and move into a place of his own. During this lengthy process he and my friend maintained a wonderfully close and enriching friendship.

Not long ago they invited me to celebrate a special occasion with them. They were married.

As I sat in the converted warehouse/sanctuary of the church where the ceremony was held, listening to the exchange of vows between a once-homeless man and a Christian friend who chose to share her life with him without reservation or condition, I wept tears of praise. I was filled with praise for a God who can truly transform lives through the simplest generosity of fellowship, through the basic offer of hospitality in Jesus' name. I was filled with praise for a God who really does raise the poor from the dust and lift the needy from the ash heap.

And wow, that must feel good!

Praise the Lord! Blessed be the name of the Lord!

Where are you, God?

Job 42:1-6

Surely all of us at some time have listened for God to speak in this world God has made. We want to hear about why things are the way they are, why soldiers rape helpless women, why parents abuse children, why people sleep on the streets, why the Holocaust ever happened and why some believe it never happened, why people starve to death every day, why someone close to us is dying of cancer.

And God's answer to us is as deafening as the silent hum of creation. "I am God. I am here. I am in control. Can't you see?"

With Job we cry out, "No, we can't see! . . . WHERE ARE YOU, GOD?"

Finally, Job confesses that God is present and is the author of all that is, and that no purpose of God can be ultimately thwarted.

But he goes a long way with his questions before he can affirm this. God help us find such a confession of hope.

The good life

James 4:13-17

⟡ Reading this passage in James reminds me of one of the more troubling and significant books I've read recently, entitled *Taking Discipleship Seriously* by Tom Sine. The book is less than 100 pages, but I constantly reread it and struggle with it. The book contains a very hard truth that I can't see how to live out yet.

Sine points out that in the New Testament, discipleship was never a "10-percent commitment" but an entire life proposition. Instead of thinking how to give up part of "the good life," we are called to fundamentally redefine what "the good life" means.

He calls Christians to radically reassess their lifestyles in light of the gospel. He challenges me to rethink my whole worldview, characterized as much by my financial investment strategies as by my desire to grow in faith. He reminds me that even as a Christian I am driven by a carefully planned calendar scheduled months, even a year, in advance—to what end? I am arrogant in my delusion of immortality.

I know what is right, though. The early church sharing everything in common, those disciples, that cross . . .

I just can't . . . not always, not my whole life . . .

God forgive me. God help me.

Tomatoes

James 5:7-11

For me there's nothing quite like a great big, vine-ripened tomato hanging on a nearly-broken branch, its shiny red skin stretched seemingly to the point of bursting, hanging next to another couple of tomatoes, not as large but just as ready to explode over the glistening black soil.

Takes a while to get to that point . . . over two long months, sometimes.

Breaking up the clods of dirt, mixing in the peat and manure, building the hills, placing the spindly little plants up to their topmost leaves almost, and then watering. Day after day after dry day, watering. Dancing when it would rain—filling the buckets or unraveling the hose when it wouldn't. And then just watching the growth take place. Just watching, Waiting. Waiting for that day when those green clusters of tomatoes would finally turn red with sunshine.

Then it was time: time to pull off those first few juice-bloated fruits from the vines.

I wash off the Sevin dust and then take a sharp knife to slice off the top. Mmmmmm . . . the seedy juice sparkles and drips over my fingers. And one by one the slices drop from my hand like round dominoes into the plate, to be salted, peppered, cut, and forked into a waiting, watering mouth.

Nope, there's nothing like waiting on God for a homegrown tomato. That's how I read James anyway.

Bearing the name

Mark 9:38-41

🕊 Come on, Lord. How naive do you think we are? Have you not flipped through the cable stations lately? Religious hucksters run amok. Charlatans grin bigger than the television screen. Greed and deception in your name continue unchecked. And casting out demons is just the warm-up for some. Do not forbid them? Surely you can't be serious. Can you really think these misguided and misleading zealots are not against you? Well, I'm certainly against them. EVERY ONE of them.

Mighty works . . . only mighty work they do is milking people's church tithes and savings . . .

Yeah, my attitude stinks. I know. I suppose that I'm against a good many things. Probably more than I'm for. But that doesn't mean I'm against you, Lord.

Of course . . . I'm not sure I'd get any reward for bearing your name, you know. I mean, if you draw too much attention to yourself you come across as self-righteous and arrogant. You know. Just like those guys on television. Besides, I'm not going to be doing any mighty works, I don't think. But I'm bearing your name as best I can. Surely somebody must take notice. I don't exactly advertise, but somebody must know I'm a Christian . . . .

I feel thirsty.

Index

Contributors

Chris Austin

Jeanne Hollifield Baucom

Linda McKinnish Bridges

LaMon Brown

Mary Caldwell

Wayne Caldwell

Bruce Calhoun

Mollie Christie

Rebecca England

Joey Faucette

Mary Anne Forehand

Carolyn S. Hale

Relma Hargus

Peggy Haymes

Alan Hoskins

Dan Ivins

Stephen Long

Roger Lovette

Jeanne Miley

Anne Thomas Neil

Mark Price

Betty Pugh

Marilyn & Bob Russell

Fred Schuszler

Layne Smith

Larry Stevens

Jon Stubblefield

Duane Toole

Helen Turlington

David Waugh

Robert E. Williams

Mary Zimmer